GLASS
LIGHT
ELECTRICITY

GLASS, LIGHT, ELECTRICITY
SHENA MCAULIFFE

University of Alaska Press, Fairbanks

Published by
University of Alaska Press
P.O. Box 756240
Fairbanks, AK 99775-6240

Cover and interior design by UA Press.
Cover image: ©Fotoworks/Benny Chan

Library of Congress Cataloging in Publication Data
LCCN 2019042706

For my parents

TABLE OF CONTENTS

ENDNOTES TO A SEIZURE

He was thinking, incidentally, that there was a moment or two in his epileptic condition almost before the fit itself (if it occurred in waking hours) when suddenly amid the sadness, spiritual darkness and depression, his brain seemed to catch fire at brief moments . . . His sensation of being alive and his awareness increased tenfold at those moments which flashed by like lightning. His mind and heart were flooded by a dazzling light. All his agitation, doubts and worries seemed composed in a twinkling, culminating in a great calm, full of understanding . . . but these moments, these glimmerings were still but a premonition of that final second (never more than a second) with which the seizure itself began. That second was, of course, unbearable.

—Fyodor Dostoevsky, *The Idiot*

One night you did not come home. Late in the morning, you pushed your bike into our apartment, leaned it against the wall, sat on the bed next to me, and confessed, finally explaining to me my loneliness. *An affair,* you said. That inflated word.

I had spent the night waiting for you. On a bench in the park, across the street from our apartment, overlooking the grain elevator. I had paced the labyrinth at the Episcopal church, meditating on being alone, on being quiet, on other labyrinths I had walked—with you, without you—on my breathing, on the importance of the exhale, on the bees hovering in the lavender. I walked uphill in the dark and the wind blew. I listened to the sounds of a couple making love in the house behind me, across the street from the overlook, their rhythm traveling so far from their open window.

Two and a half months after that night, I walked with two friends in Escalante Canyon, in southern Utah, where the river made the best trail, running between red rock walls and sky. The water was shallow and not too cold, the banks patched with quicksand that sometimes gave way beneath our weight. Our boots dangled from our packs. We wore sandals, the straps eventually rubbing holes in our skin. We covered them with moleskin and duct tape, our feet growing ever soggier. The three of us slept on a slope that was too steep for sleep (*climb high, stay out of the floodplain*). Cate, TS, and I crammed into a tent big enough for only two, all night sliding, sliding, toward the downhill end of the tent. I was the middle body, trying to stay straight, to contain myself, my arms alternately crossed over my chest or pressed to my sides. Finally, after hours of wakefulness, Cate unzipped the door, crawled outside, and wrapped herself in the rainfly—a weak barrier against ants and mosquitoes—but after that we slept a little.

The next day we walked without our packs, upriver again, but finally gave up our goal of reaching Death Hollow, which had been "just around the bend" for so many bends. We turned back. At the trailhead, we stripped out of our sweaty T-shirts and shorts and swam in our underwear, rinsing off sweat and sunscreen and citronella, getting sand in our hair.

QUICKSAND

Quicksand is a colloid hydrogel consisting of fine granular matter (such as sand or silt), clay, and salt water.

You can spot it by the way its surface quivers and shines, but usually you don't notice until you step on it and it gives way beneath you. The liquid sand pulls you down—a murky sucking at one ankle and then the other. That weekend in Escalante, we tested the depth of the quicksand with sticks, piercing it the way Odysseus stabbed and seared the eye of the Cyclops. Still, we were sometimes startled when the sand collapsed beneath us.

The night that you didn't come home I wasn't wearing my glasses, and the lights of the freighters on the dark bay, so far below, were blurry. I sent you another text message. (*Where R U? R U coming home soon?*) (*I am worried. Just tell me you are okay.*) (*Why are you doing this?*) I left another voice mail. There seemed two possibilities—which was worse? (1) Drunk, on your bicycle, you had been hit by a car. How would I find you? Should I start calling hospitals? (2) You were with K. I turned off the light. The sun was rising. Your cat curled against my body. Still it was hours before you came home. Days before the wide light of summer solstice—that vacant delirium.

The drive back to Salt Lake City from Escalante begins on Highway 12, winding along the top of a pale ridge, each side dropping hundreds of feet into the red and white canyons below. The road descends into Dixie National Forest, where the aspens are old growth and thick-trunked. TS was driving. Cate, carsick, had fallen asleep in the passenger seat.

We stopped for food in Torrey. The restaurant was called Chillerz—a standard fast-food/soft-serve grill, with windows for ordering outside and a counter for ordering inside. A few families and pairs ate at formica booths. I ordered french fries, a veggie burger, and a grasshopper milkshake.

Cate was placing her order when, behind us, a man made a sound. Or rather, a sound came out of a man who was sitting at a table. The kind of sound that makes itself. A sound that forces its way out. A sound formed by the sudden, involuntary tightening of every muscle in the body, by some lurch in the brain. I thought the noise came from a person with a disability, or with cerebral palsy, maybe. That it came from a body that often made such sounds. *Don't look.*

I sat down. TS was filling her soda. But there was a second noise. The man's friend jumped up. "Are you okay?" he asked. He didn't touch the man who was making the sounds, who was wearing leather and neoprene with kneepads and flexible elbows, like a superhero—some kind of dirt bike attire. The man groaned. His limbs moved of their own accord. His head tipped back. His legs stuck out rigidly beneath the table. His neck was taut. Someone said, finally, as if reciting a dialog in a first-aid course, "He's having a seizure. Call 911."

Still, I thought, this man probably often had seizures. People have seizures. He was probably epileptic.

"Get him on the ground," someone said. "Protect his head." But his body was stiff and sliding him out of the booth proved difficult. His head knocked against the back of the booth. (*How long does a seizure last?*) He was on the floor. Someone held his arms, which were rigid and extended. Someone cradled his head. People began to surround him. (*Don't crowd him.*)

At the counter, the woman from whom we had ordered food was on the phone. Had it happened to this man before? Was he epileptic? Had he had more than one seizure in a row?

SEIZURE

A seizure is caused by excess electrical excitement in the brain.

Seizure **1.** *The action or an act of seizing, or the fact of being seized; confiscation or forcible taking possession (of land or goods); a sudden and forcible taking hold.*

    a. *Grasp, hold; a fastening. Obs.*

    b. *A sudden attack of illness, esp. a fit of apoplexy or epilepsy. Also, a sudden visitation (of calamity).*

2. *Possession.*

3. *Mech. The action of seize.*

4. The rattle and heave of an earthquake. A crack and schism. The spark that strikes the temporal lobe. The pulse and tremble. The clutching, tensing, and grasping of the muscles. The grip and run. The rift and tremor. There's no getting around the moment of surprise.

Your confession, and our breakup, came a month after your diagnosis—*severe depression*—and the prescription—*Prozac.* In that month, you had been quieter and more equanimical. You shrugged your shoulders. You no longer kicked furniture or slammed the cupboards or shouted at the cat when he chewed papers on the desk. You pushed him off. Still, you were drinking a lot.

It was the end of the semester, I thought. The near completion of your degree. And then it was graduation—you wanted to celebrate, of course. And soon you would need to find a job, though you had already been looking for months. And then you would have to say goodbye to your friends because you would move for me, to my city and the life I had begun while we were apart (*I left you in Seattle*). It was understandable, I thought. And it was temporary.

There was a Sunday when the liquor store was closed, and we could not buy a bottle of gin. You kicked the door with the rubber toe of your sneaker.

But we had a trip planned for the solstice weekend. Mossy trails. Ocean. The long light of summer. And so many times we had imagined the house we would live in together. Soon. With a dishwasher (for you), and a garden (for me).

So I waited.

Later, in those few aftermath talks, you asked me why I let you drink so much. Why I hadn't said anything about it.

And later still I wondered (I wonder) if you recovered from your depression once I was gone. Was it a cause? Or a symptom? (Was I a cause?)

The man was still on the floor, but the seizure had passed. He was breathing loudly. (*When will it end?*) His friend said he had been in a motorcycle accident. That he was not epileptic. This information, these words, stumbled around all the bodies standing between the man on the floor and the woman on the phone. The words got lost, started over, started over again, butted against arms and mouths, finally made their way into the mouthpiece and through the wires to the ear at the other end.

The man woke up and made inarticulate sounds of panic. He tried to get up while his friend tried to calm him and pressed him to the ground.

VARIOUS TREMORS AND TREMBLINGS OF THE BODY

The body shakes to warm itself when it is cold. Shakes if it is used to alcohol in its blood and is without the usual infusion. Shakes, they say, if it is terribly afraid. Shakes after a rush of adrenaline (bicycle crash, public speaking). Shakes when overtaken by a demon. Shakes if the fatty cloak that wraps the nerves is degraded and degrading (as in multiple sclerosis or Parkinson's). Shakes if the nerves are damaged, or if it has been overwhelmed by caffeine or amphetamines. Shakes if it has been bitten by a certain spider (Australian redback, for example). Shakes if it is lacking vitamins or sleep. Shakes in anger. Shakes in orgasm.

The medical library at the University of Utah was not what I expected. No glassy, blue-green contemporary emptiness. No high, arching city view from floor-to-ceiling windows. Only old brown carpet, vacant study carrels, and a long line to pick up a book. The requested books waited on a small cart within arm's reach of the circulation clerk—there may have been fifty of them. I spotted mine easily—Owsei Temkin's *The Falling Sickness*. To the side of the check-out counter, a glass case of brain anatomy models caught my eye. One model was of a head with the skull removed. The face monochromatic, from eyelids to lips. But the brain was divided into colored sections of lavender and blue, pink, orange, green. The eyes were closed.

*

This is not the story I want (to write, to own, to inhabit).

Better to have more of the canyon. Those warm, red sandstone walls. The cottonwoods and the strange, tall birds. A coyote hunting by a stagnant pool. Yellow rock arches carved by millions of years of river water rushing and trickling, by groundwater seeping.

More about how the three of us got along—three women, like characters in a female *Stand by Me.* Our blisters and bandages. Maybe someone twists an ankle and we have to build a stretcher. We cut leg holes in a pack and take turns carrying her on our backs. Or we meet a strange river hermit who teaches us about living alone in the desert. And how I left my heartbreak there, in the river?

Or the story of the seizure—I'll detail the sounds he made, each twitch and shake, the rolling of his eyes, the drool. The three of us might get involved—I will hold the man's hand, and he will open his eyes after the shaking and take some panicked comfort in us, the three women who are helping him, speaking to him in calm, soothing voices, our long hair hanging down around him. I want us to follow the ambulance to the next town, where there is a hospital. To view the brain scans. To befriend this man who had a motorcycle wreck. To form something beautiful out of tragedy and chaos.

Or I will tell only about the breakup—about that man I've addressed here as "you." About the relationship lurking behind all this—what happened to us? What did I lose with those square hands, those blue, long-lashed eyes, those strong legs? I will track our missteps and our selfishness, reveal our equal cruelties and scars. I will reflect on the lessons I've learned. The clarity. The letting go.

But not this rolling around of language and definition. This musing and sorting. These tumbled bits.

So I witnessed a seizure. So I wish I had held that man's hand although he was terrifying, lying on the linoleum, groaning, his french fries cooling on the table.

A grasshopper-flavored shake means mint and crushed Oreo cookies. (The pun on *shake* is unavoidable but also unintentional.) The woman at the counter, who stayed so calm when the man was on the floor seizing, the woman who called the ambulance, called out that our order was ready. She was, by now, so clearly upset that Cate—who is easily affectionate—gave her a hug across the counter. The woman had a pale green milk moustache on her upper lip. She insisted that nothing like this had ever happened in their restaurant before, as if we would have blamed them for it. As if we would have thought their business a hotbed of grand mals and heart attacks and strokes.

PROPOSAL FOR CHILDREN'S SEIZURE EDUCATION

A puppet show.

Marionettes, of course.

The usual strings attached: head, hands, arms, knees, feet, thighs.

A double- or triple-cross handle, or two crosses, one for each hand.

Two puppets: Jimbo and Alfred.

Two puppeteers.

Four hands.

SHOW #1: ABSENCE (PARTIAL) SEIZURE

Jimbo and Alfred are walking home from school. It
is fall. [Drop a few leaves for a seasonal mood.] The
two puppets jump in and kick at a pile of leaves.

Alfred and Jimbo: (Improvised dialogue with laughter)

Jimbo prepares for a jump, bends at the knees. He
is a compressed spring, but suddenly he freezes.
[Jimbo's puppeteer holds as steady as possible—no
twitching.] Alfred thinks Jimbo's kidding at first,
but the pause goes on too long.

*Alfred: Jimbo! What's wrong! Jimbo! Jimbo! ~~Are you fucking with me?~~
What are you doing? That's not funny!*

Alfred reaches out to poke Jimbo. He touches him
on the arm. ~~Just before Alfred loses his shit~~—ten
seconds have passed—Jimbo resumes his jump and
lands in the leaves.

Jimbo: (laughs)

Alfred: (laughs)

Alfred thinks it was all a joke. Jimbo has no recol-
lection of the gap, has no idea anything strange has
happened.

Puppeteer: What happened, kids?

Kids (in unison): Jimbo had an absence seizure!

SHOW #2: GRAND MAL/GENERALIZED SEIZURE

Jimbo and Alfred are on the swing set. Jimbo enters the tonic phase of a seizure [Jimbo's puppeteer pulls his limbs taut.]

Jimbo: (loud groans)
Puppeteer: What should Alfred do?
Children (in unison, little voices singing): Help him lie down! Get him to a safe place!

The children are not quick enough. Jimbo has entered the clonic phase. He is shaking on the swing. Shaking and shaking, he falls to the ground, his head striking first (because heads are heavy).

Puppeteer: Faster next time, kids. Let's give it another go.

Jimbo and Alfred are eating popsicles in the front yard. They're inventing a song, singing it in a round, when Jimbo goes tonic. [Jimbo's puppeteer yanks his strings to straighten arms, legs, head.]

Kids (without prompting): Help him lay down!

Alfred helps. Flat on his back, Jimbo begins to shake. He shakes and shakes, then is still.

Kids: Check if he's breathing!

Alfred leans close to Jimbo's face. Alfred can't hear or feel any breath. Jimbo is turning blue.

Alfred: I think his tongue is blocking his airway.
Kids: Turn him on his side!

For nine months, you and I had lived in two tiny studio apartments in two different cities. But in the fall, we would give them both up and move, together, into some little house we had imagined over and over. (A quietly sloping street with trees. Gleaming wide-plank wood floors. A dishwasher . . .) But first we would spend the summer a bit crowded, in your studio, as we had spent the previous summer, after moving out of our shared apartment so I could move to Salt Lake, and return, again, to graduate school, and you could finish graduate school there, in Seattle.

The windows of your studio faced the wall of the building next door. If we looked out between the buildings, a sliver of the harbor was visible over the treetops across the street—a peek-a-boo view.

And then you stayed out all night.

In the morning you texted back. *I am fine. I will be home soon. Is the internet working?*

I pulled my clothes from the closet and piled them on the bed. I wanted to be wrong. I tried on various excuses. I gave up. I lay on the bed, waiting, watching the door.

When you pushed your bicycle into the room it seemed you were almost smiling. *Just start talking,* I said. And you did. *An affair,* you said.

Later, you told me that you had never seen me so angry. That my anger was a relief (*because it was a natural reaction? Because your own actions and reactions had ceased to feel "natural"? Because the actions and reactions of your body to another body—to a body that was not mine—were the only natural ones you had felt for some time? Whose seizure is this? Who is seizing? What is seized? I did not ask these questions. I am asking them now, but will not get answers.*)

18

The cats hid under the bed. You put your hand on my leg and I pushed it away. *Don't.*

You said you were not in love with her.

It took you such a long time to cry.

SOME FAMOUS EPILEPTICS*

- St. Paul (see below)
- Joan of Arc: The peeling of church bells triggered flashing lights and voices in her mind, driving her to heroism. Her seizures were *musicogenic*.
- Fyodor Dostoevsky: The aura was magical. A thrill. But he would have sacrificed the magic.
- Lewis Carroll: A seizure might be something like falling down a rabbit hole. And then you are too large for the world and you have overwhelming hands. Or you are too small and the table is looming. You have become a doll in the dark. You cannot climb out.
- Neil Young, Ian Curtis, Prince, George Frederick Handel, Hector Berlioz, Nicolo Paganini, Robert Schumann, Peter Tchaikovsky: Still, there is no certain connection between the brain that sparks the body to seize and a brain that composes music.
- Sir Isaac Newton: Like the apple, the body, out of water, is subject to gravity, and to the slipperiness of ice, and to seizure.
- Vladimir Lenin: Although he only suffered seizures at the end of his life, he died after shaking for fifty minutes.

* This list includes suspiciously few women.

The cover of the 1979 Joy Division album, *Unknown Pleasures,* is not, as it appears, imaging from an electroencephalogram, but a picture reproduced from the *Cambridge Encyclopedia of Astronomy,* showing the first pulsar waves ever recorded. Pulsar is what we call the waves of radiation emitted by electromagnetic neutron stars. Electromagnetism is the force that causes the interaction between electrically charged particles, the push and pull of bodies against bodies, the space between them surging and blinking.

Ian Curtis, the epileptic singer of Joy Division, who danced as if he were seizing, hung himself in his kitchen in 1980.

The *Salpêtrière* was first a gunpowder factory, and then a teaching hospital. An institution full of rats, epileptics, and the mentally ill, including, perhaps most famously, women suffering from hysteria. Does it balance the preceding list of visionary (male) epileptics that hysteria was a women's disease? All that arching and drooling, another surrender of control over one's own body? (But "surrender" implies will, and so seems at least somewhat inaccurate.) Photos from the *Salpêtrière*, where Charcot treated hysterics with hypnotism, show women giggling, their arms floating or flung overhead, long white gowns, twisted sheets, tangled hair, contorted torsos, and pale, rolling eyes. So many tongues.

What is it to be hypnotized? To surrender one's mind and body to the control of another? In that order: mind, body. And what was hysteria, now gone or renamed, vanished into other names, other diseases? The uterus, Plato said, was a drifter, blocking passageways of the body, a troublemaking creature. The uterus was the culprit. Too light, too dry, like some autumn leaf, unweighted by fluid or fetus. They begged it to return to its proper place, to anchor itself via orgasm, first by genital stimulation (*Oh, thank you, Doctor*), and later by vibrator, by water, by fans. (But I am condensing hundreds of years of hysteria into two hundred words.)

Light little womb drifting to the shoulder, lodged beneath the lung, visiting the heart. But it is all of me that wanders.

A diagram of the brain is often multicolored, so one can more easily sort the parts from each other: orange amygdala, purple temporal lobe, little pink hippocampus. The hippocampus, named for its shape (like a seahorse), is where you build your maps. Where you remember the way to the store, to your lover's house, to that tiny shop where they sell hand-cut rubber stamps. It's rumored that a London cabbie has an enlarged hippocampus, swollen with the many streets of his city.

Picturing my own city from above: so much smaller than London. My hippocampus is all sparks and buzzes thinking of that grid of streets. Follow them outward—straight lines at first, then they begin to curve in and out of each other like the whorls of an ear, ending, finally, at that those strip-mall tract-home suburbs, in cul-de-sacs. A river runs along the western edge of town, narrow on the city edge, oxbowing to the south. Cottonwoods snarl along its banks. Then the fields, in so many shades of brown or green. Farther west rises the crinkled topography of mountains, which flatten onto sagebrush, then greener plains become rows of onions, and finally, the slate gray ocean (which goes on forever).

Little is known about the hippocampus—our knowledge is mostly superstition and hypothesis—but most scientists say it's also where we store our earliest memories.

Time isn't like a river, though this is a common analogy. It might be like ten rivers, running alongside each other, braiding in and out. Ten tiny streams trickling through the fall, nearly frozen during winter, rushing during spring. I know no good analogy for time.

If I watched for a day, could I see an ice cap melting? How long does it take for the spoon to travel from the soup bowl to my mouth? How long to play a major scale? How long to let the final note linger? How long to learn to play a piece like a virtuoso? How does one keep track of rhythm? How does an afternoon spent examining rocks go by so fast? While a night at home, preparing a pot roast, and eating it in silence at the kitchen table, washing the dishes under one hissing light bulb, is endless? I toss and sweat and push the blankets to the foot of the bed. The clock glows: 11:12. 11:45. 12:33. Why did I choose the digital red over analog blue hands? It is almost the darkest day of the year.

You were in the shower. I went into the bathroom to tell you I was going outside, to the park. I spoke, you turned to face me, and I saw the shape of your body blurred, abstracted by privacy glass. You were scrubbing your penis—deliberately—desperately—a performance. It was the last time I saw you naked, if it counts. Maybe you were clothed by the hazy circles of glass. You were a voice and a familiar color of skin. The shower door had been missing hardware since we moved in. All year you had lived with that door, the manager continually promising to fix it. It was always off-kilter, always threatening to fall and break.

POSSIBLE TREATMENTS FOR SEIZURE
(Compiled and adapted from Owsei Temkin's *The Falling Sickness*)

- Slurp, simultaneously, a raven's egg and blood extracted by scar-ification.

- Consume a frog's liver. Or horse lichen. Or camel's hair, gall and rennet of seal, feces of the crocodile, heart and genitals of the hare, sea turtle blood, boar testicles, blood of the gladiator (here it is noted: this cure "falls outside professional medicine")

- Drive an iron nail into the spot where the epileptic seized, where her head first struck the ground.

- Wrap the root of a peony in linen and wear it around the neck as an amulet. Make it a fresh one, and large. This will work best if the root is gathered under a waning moon.

- Do not handle the dead—do not even touch them. (How then, does one dispose of a body? Loose ropes and dragging? Gloves? Fire?)

- Smear the patient's mouth with blood. Or bathe the patient's feet in menstrual blood.

- Kill a dog and let the patient have its bile.

- If you are the first witness of the fall, urinate into your shoe, stir the urine, and pour it into the patient's mouth.

- Wrap the victim in the skin of a goat and plunge her into the sea. Wait and see if she floats. (This tactic is for diagnosis, not treatment.)

Some seizure victims experience a physical premonition, an aura, before seizing. This may be a visual hallucination—imagined lights or blurred vision. Or it may be an acute and unexplained sense of dread or déjà vu. For others, it is an olfactory hallucination, an experience of *phantosmia*. Standing in the subway, for example, a victim suddenly smells a spring meadow or rotting flesh. When an epileptic learns to recognize the aura, it serves as a warning, giving the victim time to lower herself, time to find an open patch of ground.

An aura may be the feeling that your limbs are separated from the rest of your body. Your arm might feel as if it belongs to someone else, or is floating at a slight distance from your shoulder. *Lift my teacup*, you say to your arm, and your elbow bends. Your hand grasps the cup and lifts it to your mouth, but the feeling is as if someone else is tipping the hot liquid against your lips, and also that you are tipping the hot liquid against someone else's lips. Tipper/Tippee. Nurse/Patient.

In *The Odyssey*, people are often slackening at both knees and heart. And to die a violent death is to be "unstrung at the knees." "*I wish Helen's seed could all have perished, pitched away, for she has unstrung the knees of so many men. . . .*" Literally, this makes sense: sinew, muscle, skin, cartilage, all shriveling and disintegrating, the bones detaching from each other, dry and bare. But more than this, the phrase conjures a body like a puppet's, held together by satin thread or waxed floss or leather laces, a neat knot at the nape of the neck. One snip and the limbs detach and scatter, the bones tumbling downhill: kneecap, femur, metatarsal. Knock, knock.

Like a seizure, a shiver is an involuntary tremor, a ripple through the body, but unlike a seizure, it starts on the outside, on the surface of the body. The wind snags your arm hairs. Or her whisper strikes your eardrum. Or you walk, dripping, from the lake in the early morning, the fog rising around you (shining ghost). You squint at the brightness in the east. The air is so cold. And so your body shakes, quickly, warming itself. Your skin blooms a garden of goosebumps.

Orgasm, then, is a tremor somewhere between shiver and seizure. The source, again, begins externally, but unlike a shiver, which seems a purely physical reaction, orgasm kicks off some pretty complex brain activity. The body feels—the brain wants—the body feels. And then, at the moment of climax, we stop thinking. The body moves.

Or seizure and orgasm are opposite tremors: a seizure being an electrical spark in the brain followed by the seizing of the body, while orgasm, like a shiver, begins as friction between body surfaces. Touch is registered in the brain, circles back again to the skin, desire and friction making a continuous circuit. Or does orgasm begin (so quietly) in the brain—with the sight of the desired other? With the smell of her? I do not know where orgasm begins.

This conflation of seizure and orgasm, this epilepsy of heartbreak.

At my younger sister's wedding, a month before the night you didn't come home, you wore the boots I bought for you—brown Italian leather—and a wool vest. You had replaced the buttons yourself that morning, proud of your sewing skills. You parked the car for my dad, so my parents and I wouldn't have to walk from the lot. You held my hand during the ceremony but disappeared during the family photo session. My sister called you over. In the photos, you stand behind me, but it is visually unclear if you are attached to me or to my older sister. Then you went to get me a drink and never returned. You missed the toast and the first dance and the cutting of the cake. You danced with my sister's beautiful friend. The next morning, I woke up crying and couldn't stop, and you brought me coffee so I wouldn't have to show my puffy eyes in the kitchen, but you never asked why I was crying. No matter—I would not have been able to answer. I didn't know. You said *I need an adventure.*

Seizure victims and migraine sufferers sometimes experience "scintillating scotoma" as the aura that prefaces the seizure or headache. A black spot hovers in their vision, or lights flicker. These might expand into shimmering white arcs or zigzagging prisms. A visual hallucination.

Scintillating scotoma was first described by the physician Hubert Airy sometime during the late nineteenth century. The hovering name of a man who used words to anchor an ephemeral visual phenomenon.

Scintillate: (adj.) to sparkle or shine. "She has a scintillating personality."

Scotoma: (n.) Greek for "darkness." A blind spot. Partial degeneration of vision. In psychology, this is metaphorical, referring to an individual's inability to perceive personality traits in herself that are obvious to others.

Scintillating Scotoma: Such a sparking, sparkling darkness.

The shimmering bruise that hangs over the scene at the park. I am walking home with groceries. It is dusk, and you are still at work. Seeing a couple walking slowly, holding hands, I am startled to recognize that I am lonely. A chandelier shadow. A scrim. A warning, but I don't recognize it. (*The seizure is coming.*) (*Shimmer. Spark.*)

The taste on your lips once that I dismissed as impossible. The way you wrapped your fingers around her skinny bicep to measure its thinness—you touched her so casually, the way one touches only a body with which one is intimate, and I looked away. The dampness my fingers sought on the towels that afternoon when I came home from a weekend away—looking for proof you had slept there and woke there, proof that you had slept in our bed. The blouse I left on my pillow was unmoved, the button still loosely attached, dangling from a thread. The proof I sought that you had showered there and brushed your teeth and made coffee and fed the cats, who followed me around the apartment, meowing as if they were starving, though it was the middle of the day, nowhere near their mealtime. The towels were dry. (*I am acting crazy.*)

The blot in my vision. It was not in the sky, though I saw it there, like rising smoke. Not a lash or gnat stuck to my cornea. Not a mote or speck of dust. Not a splinter, beam, or plank. A cloud. An ink pool, floating and untouchable.

THE CONVERSION OF ST. PAUL

Saul of Tarsus hated Christians. He was on his way from Jerusalem to Damascus, where he planned to collect a few of them for trial and persecution.

As he neared Damascus on his journey, suddenly a light from heaven flashed around him. He fell to the ground and heard a voice say to him, "Saul, Saul, why do you persecute me?"

"Who are you, Lord?" Saul asked.

"I am Jesus, whom you are persecuting," he replied. "Now get up and go into the city, and you will be told what you must do."

The men traveling with Saul stood there speechless; they heard the sound but did not see anyone. Saul got up from the ground, but when he opened his eyes he could see nothing. So they led him by the hand into Damascus. For three days he was blind, and did not eat or drink anything.

—Acts 9:3–9, New International Version of the Bible

In Damascus, in a house on the Street Called Straight, Saul's sight was restored by the touch of a man named Ananias, and Saul of Tarsus became St. Paul.

A flash of light. A fall. A voice. Darkness followed by residual blindness.

In 1987, D. Landsborough published an article in the *Journal of Neurology, Neurosurgery, and Psychology* proposing that Saul's collapse may have been a seizure.

The God Helmet was constructed by Michael Persinger, a neuroscientist in Ontario. Bright yellow with black racing stripes from forehead to cervical vertebrae, studded with magnets and veined with wires that twist over the top, tangled under a strip of leather, polished beetle shell with blank snaps and a missing chinstrap, padding around the ears—a snowmobile helmet.

Sit. Relax. Close your eyes. We are attaching the electrodes. If you want to leave, speak into the microphone here, on your lapel. Okay.

An electrical pulse, stimulation of your temporal lobe, and you're gone, drifting, rising out of your body. A flickering just out of sight. God is hovering in your peripheral vision—if you could just turn your head a bit faster, a bit farther, you can't quite see Him—there, there, there. He's behind you now. A floating light. A gauzy shirt. A twinge. A scent of chopped shallots. Of cardamom. The small, bare breasts of the girl you loved at fourteen. Smoke rising into the winter sky. Yellow streetlight. Salt crystals growing in a jar. A constellation of freckles on her collarbone. The convex gleam of the eyeball. Limbs in the deep water, reaching. Sinking through a sunweb, seaweed waving. And there: your pale foot.

Many wearers report disappointment in their experience of the God Helmet. Persinger points out that one feels safe while sitting in a lab with electrodes attached to one's head, but what if you were to wake, alone, in the middle of the night, and feel yourself drifting, unmoored over the bed? What if your car stalled on a frozen road in the darkness of a Vermont January, and that light flickered, those crystals grew, you saw your body—like a sandbag, so small—sitting in the car while you floated upward with the smoke? What if you collapsed on a desert road, midday, and in the darkness that overtook your vision, there was only God flickering in the corner of your brain?

So God is an electromagnetic pulse, a spark in the temporal lobe, a hovering presence at the edge of vision. Or God built our brains to almost see him, always glimmering, always just out of sight?

I could not stay there, in your apartment, sleep beside you, pretend it hadn't happened, although I admit I wanted to. It was 3 PM. You curled on your side in bed, not looking at me. What had you expected? You said you didn't think, hadn't thought. It wasn't planned, you said. You agreed to drive me to Tacoma, to my best friend's house.

It was rush hour, a Tuesday, but I barely noticed. At the stoplight at the intersection of Denny and Dexter, where the neon pink Elephant Car Wash sign blinked and spun above us (old friend), we talked about passion. About something my mother said once about how, or why, you and I had not married. We heard an accusation. That we had not married because we lacked heat. That we lacked some essential desperation. How did she put it, exactly? You said you thought about that comment *every day*. And for a moment I thought that you were right. That she was right. That our nine years together had been useless and cold. For that moment, I forgot.

But maybe what she meant was not that we lacked passion, but that we were too concerned about timing, about circumstance, too concerned about getting things just right.

On the sidewalk, a man was walking an iguana on a leash. I pointed at him and the man bent down and picked the creature up and put it on his shoulder, and we both laughed.

For that moment, I forgot the way the wild blackberries once stained our fingertips. Their thorns caught our sleeves, scratched our ankles, drew beaded lines of blood. We lived, then, in our first house together, or rather, the first house for which we had both signed the lease, where there were no sidewalks, only gravel shoulders, and the cars parked at haphazard angles. The city felt so northern to us. The new trees. The new angle of light. How we kept saying to each other, ecstatically, *We live in Alaska!* even though it was Washington.

Once, on an island in Lake Michigan, you called me down to the shoreline, but I wouldn't come. (*Why not?*) A little exasperated, you came to where I stood, near the trees, and knelt on the stones, and asked me to marry you. But I didn't believe you. As if marriage were something you—anyone—would make a joke of, a prank on bended knee. I thought you were being impulsive. That it was a fleeting thought. That you didn't mean it. I was too surprised.

And then we didn't talk about it. The asking. The refusal. The confusion. I was about to begin graduate school for the first time, and I had this idea that it might change me, and that you were afraid of my changing, that your impulse was driven by fear. I did not say this. (*Would it have mattered?*)

And in my ears, Rilke: *poems amount to so little when you write them too early in your life. You ought to wait and gather sense and sweetness for a whole lifetime, and a long one if possible, and then, at the very end, you might perhaps be able to write ten good lines.* But I did not say this. And then, I did not change much. And those lines sound different to me now, and mean differently. There is nothing in them about being alone.

That day we rode our bicycles away from the beach, back to the ferry, in silence, you pulling ahead. I did not pedal harder.

And then, for years, you thought I did not believe in marriage, which means, at least maybe, that you understood that I loved you, or that you tried to believe that I loved you, despite what I had said (*no*) and despite what I didn't say (*I am terrified*). We were young but not too young to marry.

I didn't want to make mistakes. I made mistakes. I am making mistakes. I will make mistakes.

GLASS, LIGHT, ELECTRICITY

Our hallway was full of bicycles and dust bunnies. There was the dirt road in Idaho, the fumbling with seatbelts. The yelp of coyotes at Mono Lake. And how we got free tickets to the rodeo. In Guatemala I didn't like *tres leches* cake—so rummy and wet. The way your unwashed hair smelled like bread. It was hard to walk on a narrow sidewalk with you, beside your shoulders, just wide enough for me to read them as selfish. We were startled at the sudden green of spring sagebrush. In bed we listened to tugboats, to foghorns, to the grain elevator where the ships docked. Your back was marked by three freckles, spots on lucky dice. We carried a desk up the street for two blocks, and its edge cut into my fingers. The snowplows pushed the snow into the median. It so often rained on Sundays. You complained about your long eyelashes, how they got in the way. The bottleglass house. The redeye flight. The map room in the library. A dizzy walk across the Brooklyn Bridge. The fans in the Ethiopian restaurant spun so slowly. We cycled past a *stavkirke* and goats grazing on a turf roof. We took an all-day walk in the rain—dripping stone lions, marbles and keys and bits of old cell phones embedded in the concrete. We got lost. Woolen horse blankets on the bed. Your dead mother's St. Francis birdbath tangled in rosehips on that acre by the Rio Grande. Gray cottonwoods shook their leaves over the clothesline. While we were away, the cats turned on the faucet and flooded the house. The roads were always slick with rotten leaves. My bike tire slipped on the train tracks and I got sick with adrenaline and you put your hand on my knee and waited. Your dad raised and butchered a steer and buried the scraps in the yard. He showed me the spot. How you loved my knees. How you loved the backs of my knees. The long way you always hugged your sister. We looked into the volcano and saw only steam. At the black sand beach, you stayed so close to shore. You are not a strong swimmer. The rats on the step that we called Nimn. The ladder to the attic rooms. Calla lilies in the yard. The drunk with bare, red knees pissing in the doorway. The shower with excellent pressure. The haircut on the back step. We drank a lot of whiskey. We left our shoes in a heap by the door. We watched each other.

THE HEALING MACHINE

NEBRASKA

Maybe it was summer. Call it hazy July, 1935. Emery took a break from his mother's bedside and walked the hills. Grass and sand, roots anchoring it all so loosely, but for such a long time, and below that the aquifer, quiet and dark and invisible. In low spots the water seeped through, forming ponds and swamps. The toes of his shoes grew damp.

The cranes were his company, with their black, backhinged knees, their stalk legs and black-tipped feathers—gray, soft, and draping—their red eye patches. Had he missed them when he was away? Had he thought of them? Their long necks and those wings that could wrap a man and hold him, if only the birds were less shy? A five- to six-foot span—overwhelming. What did they sound like, the cranes? A ratcheting squawk, like something wooden was caught, rattling in their throats. And that step-step-wild hop-flap of a mating dance. The approach. The circling of the desired. The endless cavorting.

From above, nowadays: irrigation crop circles and perfectly straight roads. Nothing to go around. Nothing to go over. The sandhills roll like tumors (try again). Like goiters bubbling from the earth, but rippled and waving, those empty, endless, grassy dunes (try again). They move like pelts.

He would bury his mother there, in January. Chip away at the frozen soil of Custer County and heap it back again. And later, he would bury his father there too. Stomach cancer took his mother. Lung cancer his father.

PHOTOGRAPH #1 (circa 1972)

Emery Oliver Blagdon sits at a table. The soft, filthy brim of his cap is folded upward. Yellow light comes through the window behind him and his eyes gleam with the reflection of it. His beard, shaggy and white, overwhelms his face. Tools hang on the wall behind him. The counter is heaped with boxes and tins, loops of wires, crumpled paper, a heap of dirty rags. Squinting, you can make out the label on an old canister of Nestlé Quik. His face is tilted downward, but his eyes meet yours, quiet and certain.

By the time of this photograph, he had lost both parents and three siblings to cancer. He leased his two hundred acres to his younger brother, for farming, but he lived in the house and built his Healing Machine in the shed. When he died, in 1986, his body, too, was riddled with cancer.

PHOTOGRAPH #2 (circa 1979)

Shoelaces untied. Grinning and unbuttoned. Gray-white beard, overgrown and frizzy. Scaly elbows. Blocky brow. Thin line of hair on his chest. Suntan fading mid-sternum. His belt is buckled but the end, untucked, curls back. On his pinky he wears a thick silver ring. Wide, knobby-knuckled hands—one pressed against his stomach, the other hanging at his side. He is not wearing the copper bracelets meant to relieve joint pain (blood was thought to absorb the copper by osmosis, through the skin). Daubs of paint mark his forearms. Around him hang various wires and paper pieces of The Healing Machine.

Born in Callaway, Nebraska, in the Sandhills, Emery rode the rails during the Depression. Looked for gold in California. Visited home now and then. His eight maternal aunts and uncles were scattered across the Garfield Table in their nearly identical houses. His was a family of E's: Edward and Emma. Ethel, Emery, Edward Jr., Edna. He fixed tractors and bicycles. Built mechanical toys with moving parts for his nephews and nieces. Painted the kitchen wainscoting silver. Grew his vegetables in an unwieldy garden. Concocted peanut butter–watermelon cakes. Loved the Fourth of July and his own birthday. As he aged, his eyebrows softened and his hair grew long.

LABELS

Folk artist. Outsider artist. Self-taught. Working-class. Builder of vernacular environments. Visionary. Tramp. Naïve. Primitive. Intuitive.

He called himself a scientist. Channeling electromagnetic energy through wire and glass beads and wood and paint and scrap metal. And salt. Most important, those mineral salts.

IN *MR. WILSON'S CABINET OF WONDER*

At first all you've got is a few disconnected pieces of raw observation, the sheerest glimpses, but you let your mind go, fantasizing the possible connections, projecting the most fanciful lifecycles. In a way, it's my favorite part about being a scientist—later on, sure, you batten things down, contrive more rigorous hypotheses and the experiments through which to check them out, everything all clean and careful. But that first take— those first fantasies. Those are the best.[1]

1   Tom Eisner, quoted in Lawrence Weschler, *Mr. Wilson's Cabinet of Wonders* (New York: Vintage Books, 1995) and quoted in Leslie Umberger, "Emery Blagdon: Properly Channeled," in *Sublime Spaces and Visionary Worlds: Built Environments of Vernacular Artists* (New York: Princeton Architecture Press, 2007), 222.

DEFINITION: MACHINE

A machine is an expedient remedy. Does it necessarily have moving parts? Does it use or transfer energy? A stapler is a machine for hinging pages. An eye might be a machine. The way it gathers and condenses light. The way it flips the image. The eye is an expedient translator. Is a mattress a machine? The way its coils return equal and opposite pressure against the [resting] [tossing] body? Is it only a machine when the body presses against it? Does it make expedient sleep? Is a sweater a machine? All those interlocking fibers trapping and pocketing body heat? A bobby pin, inserted into the hole on the clothes dryer (which is certainly a machine) where the start button fell off and disappeared into its own hole, might successfully start the dryer, but there may be a few sparks. Some smoke and burnt plastic. Is a cat a machine? For its pistons and joints, its many moving parts, its sockets and tendons and claws? This transference of energy is an expedient remedy for loneliness.

COPPER IS A SOFT CONDUCTOR

Emery wore a bracelet on each wrist, copper being said to ease the pain of arthritis. He was double-cuffed. He had terrible arthritis. The fluid in his joints—where did it go? A leak somewhere and the fluid seeping out, leaving the bones, the cartilage, glancing off each other, too close. Wearing away. A knock or two. The quiet drag and scrape. Then the swelling.

AS DESCRIBED BY EDNA[2]

Sure, he wore overalls a lot, but so do most of the men around here. Sleeves rolled to the elbow. Always a button or two missing, or just left unbuttoned. He could be careless like that. Haphazard. Floppy. Maybe that's the word for it—there was a floppiness to him. After the buttons fell off his shirt he'd keep it closed just by tucking the tails into his waistband. Pants rolled in big cuffs—a little stiff cause they were so dirty. Yeah, he was always kind of dirty, but he did his own laundry once a week. I brought him a plate of food once in a while, and he ate dinner over at our place pretty often, but mostly he took care of himself. Dried his pants on the line. His beard? Yeah, well, I cut his hair for years until he got strange about it. The last time I cut his hair he fainted dead away. Fell right down on the floor in a heap. Fear, I guess. He was so afraid of the pain when the scissors cut through his hair. And he thought his hair had power. Like Samson in the Bible? When he heard the blades he just fell right over. Poor thing. That was the last time. He just let it all grow after that.

COINING THE CHARGES

It was [Benjamin Franklin] who coined the terms, positive and negative charges. He defined the negative charge as one which is similar to the charge produced by stroking hard rubber with fur, and a positive charge as one similar to that produced by stroking glass with silk.[3]

---

2   An imagined conversation, extrapolated and cobbled together from various descriptions of Blagdon.

3   In the 1970s a local teacher gave Emery a science textbook, *Matter and Energy*, by Arthur Talbot Bawden. It is from this book, a copy inscribed in cursive with the name "Edith Pritchard," that this quotation was culled.

PHOTOGRAPH #3

In the kitchen, starting at the ceiling light fixture, he painted a radiating series of red concentric circles across the room, filled with alternating green and yellow bands of color. He treated the kitchen wainscoting with silver radiator paint and the walls above with a shiny pale pink, with green half circles where those walls met the ceiling at the corners, and he detailed the light bulbs with stripes, dots, and other shapes.[4]

He baked bread. He stood at the stove, stirring a pot of soup, boiling an ear of corn. He took off his shoes. He scuffled along in his underwear.

WHILE HE WAS BUILDING THE HEALING MACHINE

Nikola Tesla was dead and had been dead for nine years, plenty of time for his orderly hair to lose the grooves of the comb, for his moustache to stop growing, and his skin to shrivel and decay and bare that thin skull. Time for the electricity of the brain to fizzle out and depart (to where? All that trickling, itinerant energy). In Emery's kitchen, the radio fizzed and popped and spoke the news to him while he baked. (Radio: a machine. Antenna extended, it captures only those waves to which it is tuned and lets the others float by uninterrupted.)

Eisenhower was elected president. Alaska and Hawaii became states. Kennedy was elected president. Kennedy was shot—the bodies in the convertible ducked and sprawled. Kennedy died. The US continued hushed entanglements in Vietnam. LBJ took over the presidency. Heaps of papers were signed (the pens, now steeped in the

4   Leslie Umberger, "Emery Blagdon: Properly Channeled," in *Sublime Spaces and Visionary Worlds: Built Environments of Vernacular Artists* (New York: Princeton Architecture Press, 2007), 205.

magic dust of history, were given away as tokens, framed and hung above fireplaces). LBJ was elected. Hushed entanglements roared. The marchers on Selma were blasted in the streets with high-pressure water hoses, yanked by arm, by leg, by neck. They were struck with billy clubs. The girls were burned in the church.

Andy Warhol had an old warehouse space—The Factory— papered with foil and spray painted silver. A good time to think silver, he said. Foil. Knife blades. Photographs. The mechanized production of Elvis, over and over.

Millions of veins were cauterized. Over twenty thousand people were lobotomized. Electroconvulsive therapy gained and lost popularity for treating depression, mania, general psychosis.

Nixon was elected. Ford became president. Carter was elected. Reagan was elected.

5

5 Nikola Tesla, with his equipment for producing high-frequency alternating currents. Wellcome Collection.

AFTER HIS FATHER DIED

Emery started tatting wires. His pretties. Twisted wire shapes that he hung side by side from another wire. Mobiles. Wind chimes. Parts of machines. Some like the coils from the insides of old mattresses. Baling wire doilies. Wrapped and knotted and dangling. In sister Edna's living room he tatted. Beside him Edna knitted.

PHOTOGRAPH #4

Rows and rows of wires. Copper wrapped boards. Waxed paper–aluminum–waxed paper sandwiches. Little scrolls of tin. Snarls and snags. Drifting squares of salvaged metal. Bright beads, glass and plastic, paint.

INSIDE THE HEALING MACHINE

He built it in the barn first, but the roof collapsed, pulled down by the pretties and nails and paint and magnets and jars. He salvaged the wood and built a two-room structure, low ceilinged, the work space and the healing space side by side.

It was kind of comical watching him do something; he'd wiggle around there awhile, [and] sometimes he'd [lay a piece] down and leave it right where it was, pick it up, and pretty soon he'd start tinkering with it again.[6]

Sometimes people said they felt it—the energy—healing them, buzzing through the wires. Your arm hairs rippled if you stood in the middle of the shed. Goosebumps rising across the surface of your skin: right arm, small of the back, up the spine, nape of the neck, down the left arm, wiggle fingers. In the soles of your feet: the hum of the earth, the soil, the heat, the aquifer. You knew it was there.

6 Ben Fox, interview by Dan Dryden, November 1987, quoted in Umberger, "Emery Blagdon," 211.

You were engulfed by twinkling lights—cheap, twisted Christmas strands—and the wood, so splintered and warm. There was the scent of paint and dirt and oil. Wire wrapped jars. The taste of copper on the tip of your tongue. Your knees loosen a bit, as if the ligaments had been untied, then retied in a floppy bow instead of a knot. Your stomach touches your shirt when you breathe, the kiss of cotton and skin cells. The buzz moves through your neck, out your skull, into the tip of each hair on your head. You might want to lie down, press your cheek to the painted board, but then, you might prefer to conduct the energy. Conduct it, as if a symphony, the flutter of electrical current coursing through your raised arms, the braided energy of the earth passing through your hands and out the end of your baton, filling the room. You, a lightning rod.

Maybe it was Emery's energy they felt—the hours he put into painting the wooden panels with those muted bright colors, gluing beads to the panel, twisting, twisting, wire after wire after wire, attaching this bent fork, that tin plate, hanging a vial of salts, emptying crystals onto a glue-smeared board. Bending a coat hanger. Cutting his thumb on the jagged edge of a can. Mousetrap, pie tin, baling wire, ribbon, and wax circuit board.

But some people felt nothing. They saw the paint on the boards, the light glinting against glass and wire, the spinning, sharp-edged tops of coffee cans. And they felt nothing.

HE WENT TO THE PHARMACY
He said, "I'd like to buy some elements."

He was so intent on his inquiry that I took him seriously—which, to look at the man, you wouldn't really. "Elements" is a broad category, I thought. I tried to ask him what kind of elements he wanted, what he was doing with them. He said he was building machines—magnetic machines—machines that had electrical activity. So I thought the only elements I know, per se, having any electrical activity are simple earth salts—mineral salts. This guess turned out to be accurate . . . I offered to give him some. I went back to my wets-and-dries counter and filled up various vials with these powders—salt powders, crystals, sodium chloride, maybe some sulfur and a few other inorganic compounds. I labeled these—he was very happy to receive these. His face brightened up, and he was getting very talkative.[7]

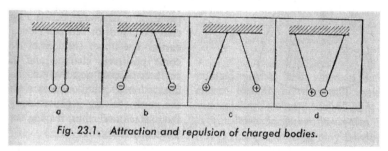

Fig. 23.1. Attraction and repulsion of charged bodies.

[8]

7   Dan Dryden, "Emery Blagdon Recollections," 1987, quoted in Umberger, "Emery Blagdon," 211.

8   From Arthur Talbot Bawden, *Matter and Energy* (New York: Henry Holt and Company, 1957).

THERE WAS A GIRL ONCE

She lived on a neighboring farm, but her father didn't approve of Emery. His vagabonding. His sixty-mile-per-hour tractor. The way he loitered at the soda fountain and didn't work that much. The man didn't know responsibility, and besides, the way the children liked him—wasn't it a little creepy? But they liked him for fixing their bikes, for asking them questions, for catching lightning bugs with them, in jars, and after they fell asleep beside that lantern of bugs, Emery always let the bugs out. When they woke, the jar was open and empty. The bugs were off sleeping, or doing whatever it is that lightning bugs do during the day when their lights don't shine against the darkness.

ETHEL DESCRIBES THE HEALING MACHINE

He invited her into the machine, of course. *Nothing doing,* she said. *I didn't want to go in there. It was a lot of wires and stuff.*[9]

ITINERANT IS A HARD WORD

Metallic and knocking. It is often applied to traveling preachers, but means, more generally, moveable. One who roams. Does the wanderer have a home somewhere? Some place that holds him? That he thinks of when he is away? Is he always trying to return, or is he trying to escape? He is always longing for another place.

Try *vagabond.* Why does he leave? Over and over, he is always leaving. Does he lose track of himself, leaving a fragment in each place—an eyelash in Nashville, a tooth on the boxcar, his gullibility in San Francisco? Or is he overwhelmed by the places he takes with him? Such heavy baggage: the green ocean wave, the beckoning

---

9 Ethel Blagdon Sivits, interview by Don Christensen, October 1990, quoted in Umberger, "Emery Blagdon," 208, but sonically adjusted here.

51

limbs of the Joshua tree, the pale child offering her glass of lemonade, the bed with cool white sheets, the gray morning light and a pillowcase printed with yellow roses that smelled of another's hair? Is his body his only home?

Try *nomad*. Is the firmest self the one independent of opinions? Free from conversations that thread years? From the expectations of other people? Is the firmest self the one that washes away? The one who says: *There is no self?*

Try *hobo*. He collected places like Easter eggs.

ON THE QUALITY OF LIGHT SURROUNDING THE AVERAGE MACHINE

Cold. Mechanical. Inhuman and, possibly, inhumane. Think robot, for example, and likely you think silver, cold-toned. But the Healing Machine was copper and gold and bronze and—yes—silver, too. Glinting. The wood was old and streaked and maybe half rotted. Paint, wood, warm-toned metals, the yellowy twinkle of Christmas lights, the wax-paper-like layers of skin, like a well-peeled sunburn.

(But what about the cotton gin? What about the printing press? Those are machines and they are not cold-toned or metallic. What about the way you want to eat the letterpress stamps, or more, to press them to your skin, wear an "R" in Garamond on the soft inside of your wrist, an "E" in Palatino Linotype on your cheek?)

WHAT THE CITY SAID

He refused to cut his hair and paid little attention to what he wore. He looked like a scary old vagrant. Now he can be seen as a great rural American shaman.[10]

10   Ken Johnson, "Emery Blagdon: Flights of Fancy from the Artist as Medicine Man." *New York Times,* January 10, 2008.

OTHER MACHINES: THE MODIFIED SNOOPERSCOPE [11]

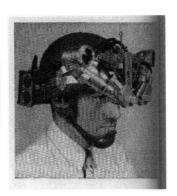

Fig. 31.2. A modified version of the snooperscope tube to give binocular vision for night driving. It runs off of the vehicle's power system. (Radio Corporation of America.)

HE PICKED UP ODD JOBS

The sawmill and the lumberyard smelled of sawdust and sometimes a little like burning wood from the friction between buzzing blade and board. A little oil kept things turning smoothly and occasionally smelled like popcorn. Emery wondered aloud: is sap tree blood? Sawdust collected around his nostrils. He blew opaque white snot onto his handkerchief, stuck it back in his pocket. He wore gloves but the splinters dug into his flesh anyway, festering, pink and swollen, blotching his forearms and the skin between fingers. Tweezers were useless. Edna squinted through a pair of reading glasses and pushed at them with a needle. Emery squeezed his eyes shut. If a tree could grow from a sliver, he thought. If a tree could grow from his arm it would be worth it. A tender-rooted sapling ready for transplant. A new solution of sap-blood in his veins.

Baling hay was no better. Still the scratches on his arms. The grass was named timothy. The hot dust in his eyes. The men whistling and opening lunch pails. He whistled too, looping and low. Windmills cut the sky with their bony limbs. Their flayed fingers

11   From *Matter and Energy,* Arthur Talbot Bawden. Henry Holt and Company, New York. 1957.

53

sliced and gathered wind. And down in the dirt, the water pumps nodded. Prayed to mud and grass and spit their bounty into ladles, into pails and troughs. For lunch, he had two chicken wings and a leg, and a wide slice of rhubarb pie.

ON HAIR AND OTHER INANIMATES

Hair was dead, of course, and brainless, but he feared for it nonetheless. That the snip would hurt it. All that energy that would escape from the cut, invisible, but gushing like blood from a wound, electricity from a live wire. Feared that *things* had feelings.

He considered the sensitivity of a piece of pie, the crust separated from itself, the juices running. Of the broken shoelace, gray and fraying, marked by the black rings of metal eyelets. Of a page no longer blank, its surface scratched by a pen running dry, the marks accumulating, pressing faintly through to the other side. The communion between the wire and his swollen joints. In everything a sensate buzz.

The human body walked through the world like a spindle, the invisible energy winding upon it, tighter and tighter. Like the sputtering fuse on a stick of dynamite. To feel oneself as the spindle, or as the circuit between aquifer and sky. To live in the space between catgut and fret, absorbing the vibrations. This was the purpose of The Healing Machine. To shake loose the pain, to carry it to the next thing, to release it, but also to be the knot, the fuse, the loosened gnarl.

MILES AND MILES OF NOTHING

There was the house, faded gray in the yellow grass. There were the cornfields. In the dark, crickets. In the day, cicadas and rustling. The front steps were flanked by two overgrown junipers. Musk thistle and small, twisted sunflowers tangled along the walk. An eastern red cedar half blocked the steps.

Emery, Edna said. Your house looks abandoned.

Anyone who mattered would know to go around back, he said. Or knock on the door of The Healing Machine. And they did. They knocked. They waited.

Afternoons in summer the sky turned green. Tornadoes. Hail. But when the lightning storms blew through most nights in July, Emery watched the strikes roll across the hills, marching toward him, forking and flashing. He felt them in his hair, in his fingers, in the copper bracelets around his wrists. The buzzing heat in his throat and in his knuckles. The crickets and bats fell silent. The cattle pressed against the barbed wire and lowed. Their coarse hides prickling. They bellowed and the rain fell on them. A loose board banged somewhere out back. The curtains snapped but he never bothered to close the windows. He liked the puddles under his feet in the morning.

PHOTOGRAPH #5

A newspaper photo. Blurry and cropped to a portrait. A laughing cloud of beard fills the dark frame. Pixelated wrinkles. And his eyes—where, in the other photographs you see the spark—are lost. Is he wearing glasses? Over and over, the accompanying article calls him "The Old Farmer."

THE BODY IS NOT LIKE A PHOTOGRAPH

Simplified, the aura of a work of art is that clingy trace of the maker, the non-mechanical quality, like a halo, the smudge of human-ness. We can print photograph after photograph and they will look identical. The body is a closed system of one-way roads. Every penis exactly the same when it comes down to the two tiny veins, pinched off when the arteries rush. But the small intestine, framed by the orderly large intestine, loops everywhichway, a different bouquet in every body, a haphazard mess of ruffles. The small intestine is unique in its heaping.

Machines that read the output and rhythms and shorted circuits of the body: The X-Ray. The ultrasound. The blobs of color on a nuclear image, marking the place where the blood slows and gathers, indicating the clogged artery at the entry to the heart. The seismic blips of the EKG.

Emery avoided doctors. Did he feel the tumors gathering within him? Like cumulous clouds, all billow and rise? Did his arthritis go into remission, his body distracted, producing something new? Each day he pressed his cheek to the painted boards of The Healing Machine. Each day standing perfectly still, feeling the twinge and the currents.

CONSIDERATION: HEALING

1. Skin knits itself together and scabs over.
2. The scab falls off, leaving behind a purplish spot.
3. Scars are also called cicatrices.
4. We opt for the easy term which is less beautiful and more closely resembles its sign. "Scar" slices and steams when spoken.
5. The body heals around shrapnel when necessary.
6. The heart reroutes the blood if the usual route is defective. Say you were born without a particular artery. If you are lucky the lub-dub will go on. The body improvising.
7. It is the overproduction of collagen that leaves a scar.
8. Smear it with vitamin E.
9. After gastric bypass the skin remains six sizes too large, draped over the shoulders, dewlapping the triceps, skirting the body.

10. You want to heal, but to heal means to incorporate the shrapnel, to minimize the overproduction of collagen.

11. Who wouldn't want to feel the vibrations, the electrical currents?

12. A suture, too, leaves a scar.

13. A Band-Aid is a plastic suture. You get to peel it off. The sticky black outline of lint stuck to glue is not a scar because it washes off.

14. Cauterization. Amputation. These, too, "heal."

THE MAKER IS NOT CLUMSY

Emery hammered at a piece of tin, denting it flat. He punched a couple of holes in the corners and stuck a bit of wire through. He changed his mind, pulled the wire out. The holes remained. He looked up at Edna who was standing in the doorway. "Dinner," she said. "If you want it." She was holding a plate with a pile of greens and cooked carrots and meat. He stood up and wiped his hands on his pockets. He took the plate from her. He said, "Crumpled tin will never look new again, no matter how you press it and smooth it."

THE PHARMACIST ON THE HEALING MACHINE

It depends upon what you mean by healing powers. If you mean is there an emotional, psychological impact that can affect your outlook, I would say yes, it definitely has powers of some kind.[12]

WHO IS HEALED?

The maker? The looker? The writer? The one who stands absolutely 100 percent motionless on the painted, salt-smeared panel? Right

12 Dan Dryden quoted in Joe Duggan, "The Healing Machines of Nebraska," *Lincoln Journal Star*, January 7, 2006.

here: under these twisted wires. Under this chandelier of painted baby food jars and plastic beads and copper coils. Right here: where the energy fields converge.

Emery hopping in excitement: Stand here, he said. Do you feel it?

POSSIBLE MACHINES: THE SCENT DISTILLER
A small copper pot—about two inches round—that collects an air sample, then distills and concentrates the scent of that parcel of air. These scent molecules are compressed into a tiny block, like a bouillon cube, and vacuum-sealed. To regenerate, add water and simmer over low heat.

Air Scent Sample distilled in Salt Lake City, Utah, at 1001 E. South Temple on November 21, 2010: Salt, algae, sulfur, car exhaust, coal dust, copper, copper by-products (mostly alkaline soil), leaf meal, cut grass, soiled kitty litter, singed hair, cooked pork, spearmint chewing gum, lavender, sweaty gym socks, coffee, rubber of a bicycle tire, bicycle chain lubricant, Simple Green biodegradable cleanser, cedar soap, dirty wool (how long will you leave that pile of clothing before taking it to the cleaners?).

Air Scent Sample distilled in Callaway, Nebraska, at the corner of Third and Main on July 13, 2011: Crane excrement, Sunflower pollen, corn pollen, nitrate fertilizer, Roundup Ready, diesel, popcorn, car exhaust, paper pulp, cattail, burnt matches, asphalt, wet concrete, sweaty gym socks, coconut sunscreen, pine sap, tarpaper, varnish, apple pie potpourri, paraffin, honey-baked ham.

A RIDDLE IS A CONUNDRUM OR ENIGMA

By the time Emery died, his body was riddled with tumors. The doctors guessed they had been growing for ten years. That grain of sand in the oyster, growing precious. Then a rhizome with running roots spidering the soil. A potato with so many eyes. The doctors had not seen him in town. Not at the clinic. His only medicine had been The Healing Machine.

THE PHARMACIST, DRIVING[13]

The high school class reunion was in North Platte, twenty miles west. Dan and his high school friend Don sped along I-80, the fence posts stuttering past like a film. Dan's hands at ten and two.

It had been years, Dan said. What—six or eight? Since he had given Emery the elements and then, curious, driven out to the hills to check out The Healing Machine. That way somewhere. (He took a hand from the wheel, gestured at the hills). Maybe ten miles north. Just this totally unassuming shack. You'd never know from looking at it.

The interstate cut a corridor between the hills.

We should stop, said Don. You've been telling me about this kook and his magic salts for years. The G and T's will wait.

Yeah? You want to? Dan said.

There was no one at the farm. The hem of a kitchen curtain was pinched in the window sash, flipping in the wind. They walked up to the porch. A bill was posted on the door.

Emery Blagdon had died. The estate would be auctioned. The woodstove. The windmill. Lots of fancy wire work. Some painted boards. Some Jars. Homemade toys. Pie tins. Paints. The list was long—the Healing Machine would be sold piecemeal. More than four hundred individual components.

13   An imagined conversation.

THE GAVEL AND THE AUCTIONEER

Each shining jar of salt held like a scope against the sky.

Andwe'vegotsomemorewires.What'llyougiveforthesewires.CanI-getfifteen?Fifteen.SeventeenSeventeen.Twenty.Twenty.Twentyfive.
AndTwentyfive.Thirty.Thirty?Thirty.CanIgetthirtyone?Goingonce-atthirty.Twice.Soldforrthirty.Andwe'vegotanotherboxofjars.

Dan Dryden and his friend Don Christensen purchased the Emery Blagdon works at the sale of his estate in 1986. They bought all four hundred pieces. The shed was torn down.

PHOTOGRAPH #6

A man and woman, wearing green latex gloves, tinker with a piece of The Healing Machine balanced on a table. Fluorescent light and gray industrial carpet. They bend their heads. They wield brushes and tweezers. They breathe mint and wear aprons. They do not look up for the photograph.

SOURCE NOTE

Throughout the entirety of this piece I have quoted, stolen from, and merciless-ly appropriated words and information from Leslie Umberger's remarkable essay, "Emery Blagdon: Properly Channeled" from her book *Sublime Spaces and Visionary Worlds: Built Environments of Vernacular Artists* (New York: Princeton Architectural Press, 2007). I credit her with most of the information found here and with none of the inventions, fabrications, mistakes, misquotes, or careless imaginings. I am an unreliable source, making various assumptions and projections, imagining scenes and conversations based on small factual details. You can put these pages down, but the words will still be here, the ants parading. My voice, their voices, stored in ink or electricity. I am no scientist. I am barely responsible enough to pay my cell phone bill on time.

TEN ON POISON

1. ALL THINGS ARE POISON

According to Paracelsus, whose written works include *On the Miners' Sickness and Other Diseases of Miners*, "All things are poison and nothing is without poison. Only the dose permits something to be not poisonous." *Botulinum*, for example, was once the killer lurking in a dented can of beans but is now used to smooth crows' feet and shore up a sagging chin. Other poisons include champagne, cherries, chocolate cake, mercury in fish, particulates in the air we breathe. When bothering with the nitty-gritty of terminology, toxicologists differentiate between *poisons* and *toxins*. Toxins are produced biologically, while poisons are derived chemically and absorbed through the skin or the gut. Both will wreak havoc in an organism, be it an outbreak of hives or be it death.

2. THE GENEROUS GASTRONOME
(JOHANN SCHOBERT SPEAKS)

The jack-o'-lantern mushroom is often mistaken for the chanterelle but can be easily differentiated by its perfect gills. But the jack-o'-lantern is lovely! Oh succulent, oh glowing fruit of the forest floor! I have plucked the jack-o'-lantern and cooked it with butter, garlic, a splash of wine, and let me tell you: it was delicious. The first time I ate just a nibble—taking the tiniest morsel on the tip of my fork.

I chewed. I swallowed. I waited. I did not die. I took another bite. I returned to the forest and filled my satchel. Tonight my family and I shall have the most delicious feast. Mushroom hunters are a devious bunch, selfish and crafty. Those who warn you off this most tasty fungus, they are only hoarding the feast for themselves.

(And while I am busy correcting misnomers . . . *If* my compositions are so easy for your children to play, Leopold Mozart, it is only because your children are of unnatural musical ability and not because my compositions are simple, as you have implied. That Wolfgang of yours—he *will* amount to something.)

3. FROM THE DICTIONARY OF POISON

Atropism: to die after consuming belladonna, that droopy purple flower I learned to call Deadly Nightshade when walking in the woods as a child. A drop in each eye will dilate the pupils, an effect once considered beautiful, no matter that it may also cause blindness over time. It seems we've outgrown the use of belladonna for sparkling eyes, but we haven't outgrown our attraction to sparkling eyes. I use eyedrops too frequently, in part because my eyes are dry and burning, and in part because they contain naphazoline, a vasoconstrictor, shrinking the branching veins, brightening the whites so my eyes shine more greenly, like they did when I was younger. If I used these eyedrops ten times a day, would they become poisonous? It's likely my eyes would no longer be able to regulate their own moisture or vasoconstriction, but is this *poison*?

Enriositatis: a habitual state of drunkenness, the blood oversaturated, poisoned by alcohol, but the word also conjures drowning in a river. Once, I picked up a friend for an unplanned afternoon. She was terribly hungover, which surprised me because she so often drank to drunkenness. Anyone, especially someone drinking for the first time, can get sick from alcohol, but I thought the habitual drinker rarely suffered a hangover, instead maintaining a low level of alcohol in the body at all times. In the thrift store, where my friend and I were searching for plastic dolls we could cut up and piece together into a nuclear disaster babydoll, my friend rushed outside and vomited onto her T-shirt. We went for lunch. She was very quiet. I found myself babbling over my eggplant lasagna, such poisonous, empty words. I did not know what to say or how to help.

Iophobia: an exaggerated fear of poisons. Io is a black-spotted moon of Jupiter, named after a lover of Zeus. A poisoned moon, dappled with decay.

Plumbism or *Saturnism:* a poetic name for lead poisoning, about which there is nothing poetic. Lead in the blood makes a person angry, lowers the IQ. Skin laced with metal. Heavy purple veins. A baby has an uncanny ability to see small things because they contrast with their surroundings. How she reaches for the cheerio, for the button, for the flake of paint on the floor. She puts everything in her mouth.

Urotoxy: measures the toxicity of urine. How concentrated must it be to kill the one who drinks it?

4. THE POISONOUS UMBRELLA:
THE STORY OF GEORGI MARKOV[1]

It was raining a fine, incessant mizzle. Georgi Markov, exiled to London, shuffled across the Thames to catch his bus. He turned up the collar of his coat, tucked his briefcase more tightly beneath his elbow. He checked his watch and tapped his foot, anxious even though he had plenty of time.

He felt a jab in his calf.

Georgi yelped. Something had bitten through his slacks! Something had bitten him in the leg!

A tall woman in a gray trench coat stood before him, a belt cinched round her waist, huge black sunglasses sliding down her nose. She mumbled an apology: her clumsiness, her poor vision. Her head was wrapped in a chartreuse scarf, but a few blonde hairs had escaped and clung to her temples. She inspected the tip of her umbrella, which Georgi saw was marked with his blood. His blood! On the tip of her umbrella! The woman took out a tissue and wiped the

---

1   Markov was a Bulgarian writer, a dissident who defected to Italy in 1969 and later moved to London. Markov worked for the BBC, broadcasting his "In Absentia Reports," continuing his criticism of the Bulgarian Communist government. In 1978 Markov died after allegedly being shot in the calf with a small metal pellet, the shot apparently fired from the tip of an umbrella, though according to the Berlin Spy Museum, even this detail may not be true. It is more likely that the ricin-filled pellet found in Markov's leg after his death was engineered to melt at 37° C, the temperature of the human body, and was shot into his calf from a separate, hand-held device and that the umbrella was merely a distraction. The detail was reported by Markov when he described the incident at the hospital. The suspected killer, enlisted by the KGB, who filed information about Markov under the name "The Wanderer," is Francesco Gullino—not the blonde woman of my imaginings—and he still roams freely throughout Europe. The story is good enough—great enough and tragic—that it needs no fictional embellishments. Beyond a childhood steeped in Carmen Sandiego, I have no justifiable reason for having changed the killer into a woman in glasses and a scarf in the tale above. I am so often guilty of poisoning history.

umbrella clean, then loped off, leaving Georgi to inspect the hole in his calf, which was burning something awful.

What was he to do? Georgi continued on to the office, climbing aboard his bus, sweating beneath his coat, but soon he found himself in the hospital instead. Our hero died that very afternoon. The doctor dug a tiny silver pellet out of the wound and dropped it into a vial for lab analysis.

5. ALLIUM CEPA

When you cut into an onion, two chemical reactions take place. First, the knife slices through the skin and breaks all those miniscule cells; the enzymes release a strong odor. (*My god, you should sharpen that thing. Don't you know a dull knife is a dangerous knife? You'll lose the tip of your thumb, at least.*) Second, the onion releases *allicin*, a volatile sulfur gas that irritates the eyes. (*Hold steady now. Hold steady.*)

A sharper cut will keep your eyes drier. You might try slicing under running water, or wearing goggles.

6. AIR HUNGER

During World War I, the Germans crept across the plain dressed like deep-sea divers, in canvas suits with glass lenses between their faces and the world. Sometimes chlorine clouds are described as yellow-green. Sometimes as greenish-white or pale green. Anything metal was instantly tarnished: coins, buttons, safety pins. Men died gasping, drowning in fluids produced by their own destroyed lungs.

Soldiers learned to stuff damp cloths into their mouths. The first respirators were flannel soaked with soda, but eventually a man runs out of soda. They soaked their socks in urine. They pressed their mouths to the dirt. Open mouths. Closed mouths. Their bodies tipped like sandbags.

The Hague Declaration of 1899 outlawed the use of poison gas in warfare. Chemical weapons were deemed too cruel, but of course that didn't mean the end of them.

Gerhard Schrader discovered tabun when looking for phosphorous-based insecticides. The tiniest drop and he needed three weeks to recover.

To die by tabun. To die by sarin gas. First, your pupils constrict to pinpricks. You can't read by electric light. (As if you might be trying to read, sitting beside a lamp, with Tolstoy or Steinbeck open on your lap.) You can't drive, either, in all that perceived darkness. And then, you can't breathe well. You asphyxiate. You foam at the mouth, blind within minutes.

If we are shot, we might press cloth to a wound. If we are cut, we can wrap a tourniquet. If we ride in the back of the ambulance, we might have time to narrate our death. *This is what it feels like to die.* But if you're writhing, you're not narrating. And still, poison is scarier.

The bullet, the mortar: they destroy the body locally. But gas is in everything and takes everything. Sight. Air. Control of every part of your body. Vomit, froth, diarrhea, bleeding, choking, seizing, spasming.

But death comes swiftly. There is no need, even, to breathe. Sarin enters the body through the skin, by osmosis.

7. THE MONK THAT WOULDN'T DIE

Grigory Rasputin poisoned history. It is difficult to make sense of the documents. In photos, he looks greasy and smart: long stringy hair, unruly beard, pale eyes. They say he lived through gunshots that penetrated his skull. Poison in his blood. Stabs to his abdomen. Water in his lungs. And when, finally, he died, they say his body, dead for a month, sat straight up in the flames.

Sweet cakes and wine with cyanide: the poison in his blood could have killed four horses, but it didn't kill Rasputin. They say he had a thirteen-inch penis. They say he had hundreds of lovers. *Sin,* he (may have) said, *is the way to God. Sin,* he (may have) said, *keeps a man humble. Bring me another glass of wine, why don't you? And you, my dear lady, have the most beautiful hands.*

A prostitute stabbed him in the gut and left him holding his own entrails. *I have killed the anti-Christ!* she (may have) shouted in the street. But he survived. He ate the poisonous cakes in the basement of a palace. They shot him with silver bullets (silver to kill a vampire). His body lay on the rug and the men left the room, but when they returned, he sat up and lunged at them. He wrestled. They cut him. They sawed off his mythical member. They tied his arms with ropes and tossed his body in the frozen Neva.

When his waterlogged body was pulled ashore the ropes were gone. His arms were stretched upward, his fingernails rubbed to nothing and bloody. He lost his battle clawing against a ceiling of ice. Finally, the autopsy said, it was water that poisoned him.

His daughter, Maria Rasputina, was a dancer. *There's just no way he ate those cakes,* she (may have) said. *After the thing with his entrails he suffered from hyperacidity. He avoided sugar.*

They burned his body and the autopsy report disappeared.

8. MY COUSIN'S DOG

Jack's dog, Thistle, was poisoned at the property line. A generous helping of ground beef heaped on fine china and sprinkled with rat poison. Then came the dragging of hindquarters, the panting, the hypovolemic circulatory shock, the exhaustion, and collapse.

Thistle was the offspring of my own childhood dog, a liver-and-white English springer spaniel named Freckles. The pick of the litter,

Thistle was an eager hunter with curly ears and a large brown spot on her nose.

Rat poison contains an anti-coagulant. The blood thins and thins until the animal dies from internal bleeding. These are tasteless and odorless poisons, and their power is delayed. A rat, being a scavenger, will taste the tiniest bite of its food, then wait. If it doesn't get sick, it eats more. But a dog gobbles her meal, slobbering and pushing the food around the dish with her nose and tongue.

Jack, age ten, watched Thistle collapse in the grass. He found the plate days later, floral-patterned and edged with silver, nestled in ivy, licked clean and gleaming.

9. THE WALLS STILL MARKED WITH BLUE

Hydrocyanic acid was useful for saving citrus: grapefruits in Florida, lemons in Spain, oranges in California. The crops were fumigated so the people could go on eating the fruits all winter long. On Christmas Morning, all the tables held sugared grapefruit halves. A maraschino cherry placed at each center was a candied kiss.

Hydrocyanic acid is better known as Prussian acid, derived from the same substance as that blue pigment in traditional blueprints, Prussian blue. But it is also a debugger and delouser. From there, it's a flea's leap to Zyklon B, enhanced hydrogen cyanide.

Freight trains arrived at the US-Mexico border packed with Mexican immigrants. Their clothes and bodies were misted with Zyklon B as they entered the US. Even those who walked across the border daily—to clean houses, to feed children—were doused in gasoline. These practices continued into the 1950s.

In Nazi concentration camps, 95 percent of the Zyklon B was used for delousing. The other 5 percent was condensed into wooden pellets and stored in airtight canisters until the moment it was dropped through vents into the gas chambers. An SS doctor, Johann Kremer, testified after the war:

> *The shouting and screaming of the victims could be heard through the opening and it was clear that they fought for their lives . . . When they were removed, if the chamber had been very congested, as they often were, the victims were found half-squatting, their skin colored pink with red and green spots, some foaming at the mouth or bleeding from the ears.*[2]

Maybe a third of the people, those standing closest to the vents, died immediately. There is nothing I can say about this to redeem anyone. There is no redemption from this.

Stop.

10. AS A BOY, HE HID NEITZSCHE'S BOOKS UNDER THE BED

Ethan dumps sugar in his coffee, eats bread pudding for lunch, then gets up and buys us each a second cup of coffee and a sugar cookie, frosted thick with buttercream.

Ethan wears conspicuous, expensive shoes. He carries pencils and a sketchbook, has a keen ear for overhearing interesting dialogue on the bus. He once served on a Mormon mission but eschews all that now: the companions, the restricted reading list. But he used to love to debate theology.

The German word *gleichgueltig*, he tells me, is normally translated as "indifference." *Gleich* meaning "same," and *gueltig* meaning

---

2 Quoted in Yisrael Gutman and Michael Berenbaum, *The Anatomy of the Auschwitz Death Camp* (Bloomington: Indiana University Press in association with the United States Holocaust Memorial Museum, 1994), 163.

"valid" or "value-laden." The same value. But Ethan thinks it means more than that. That it conveys something more despairing.

"If all options are equally valuable," he says, "what consequence is there in choosing? Or in not choosing?"

Heroin, he says, made all things the same, and all equally uninteresting. For three years, he did not care for his body or for other people. He kept his job. He did not seek love or sex. He did not suffer heartbreak. Time continued to pass, of course, but if he got high, it didn't matter—time or its passing were neither good nor bad. There was nothing he could do about it, and so what, anyway? Every night he went home, got high.

Six months clean this time, three months out of rehab. But if you've relapsed once, why not again? You can always check into rehab again, although it's expensive, and there is always the chance that you might die first, and the likelihood you'll fuck someone over in the process.

He stirs sugar into his coffee and takes a sip. He gestures insistently, spoon still in hand. "I saw a junkie helping this very old woman at the pharmacy. It was so obvious what was happening. First I thought, *Why isn't anyone doing anything about this? Why isn't anyone stopping this from happening?* The woman was saying, *I don't know where my house is. Do you?* I was angry. It was so goddamned obvious. He'd clean out her wallet and take her prescriptions. But I wasn't stopping it, either. And then I was angry that I'd never thought to try it myself. And how easy it would be to give in now. To slide over. My body wants it—or is it my brain? So hard to tell. But the junkie and the old woman left the pharmacy together. She was holding his arm at the elbow."

On the other side of the window, it is spring, petals blowing in bright gusts.

When we cooked dinner together, Ethan licked his fingers after chopping garlic, one at a time, extravagantly, flamboyantly. But this was not a man who I should love. Love, too, can be poisonous. I resolve to only see him in public places, to hold myself accountable (though I will fail).

A car parks in front of the bakery, and the sun off its windshield flashes on Ethan's face, highlighting two scars on his chin, dime-sized and pink, but the brightness makes him look young and boyish too.

Can restraint be poisonous?

All things, said Paracelsus. All things.

THIS HUMAN SKIN

Whenever a Scythian slays his first man he drinks some of his blood. He brings the heads of all those he slays in battle back to the king, and by bringing back a head, he receives a share of whatever plunder has been taken . . . He flays the head by first cutting in a circle around the ears and then, taking hold of it, shaking off the skin. He then scrapes it out with an ox's rib and works the skin in his hands until he has softened it, after which he uses it as a handkerchief, which he proudly attaches to the bridle of his horse. And he who displays the most skin handkerchiefs is esteemed as the best man. Many Scythians make cloaks to wear from the skins by stitching the scalps together like shepherds' coats.

—Herodotus, *The Histories, Book IV*

1.

In 1864 Robert McGee, a child, was scalped by Chief Little Turtle.[1] McGee lived and grew up with his head scarred like a baseball. Little Turtle left enough hair at the front of his head that a hat would have covered the bald spot and scars.

---

1 Henry Inman, *The Old Santa Fe Trail: The Story of a Great Highway* (London: Macmillan, 1898); Project Gutenberg, 2005).

2

Scalping seems a feat more easily accomplished on a dead victim, or with the help of an accomplice. Scalping a live person, even a child, must demand more skill, more strength and coordination. A steadier hand. But then, McGee was probably terrified. An orphaned child of pioneers, he was too young to join the army. Instead, he was hired to drive a wagon along the Santa Fe Trail. Maybe he didn't even fight, hoping that the tax of his scalp would pay for his life. Maybe he remained perfectly still while Little Turtle held him down in the dirt and cut so slowly, so carefully, like a surgeon, like a woman tracing the outline of her lover's lips, and Little Turtle tugged and tugged and pulled loose that round disk of skin, that shining tuft of pale hair.

"Little Turtle." In English a diminutive name, but in Miami-Illinois it probably named the Midland Painted Turtle, a colorful species that played trickster. *Michikinakoua*[3] was a war chief of the Miami. Eventually he begged his fellow Indians not to fight white

2   Robert McGee, scalped as a child by Sioux Chief Little Turtle in 1864. Photo by E. E. Henry. Library of Congress Prints and Photographs Division, https://lccn.loc.gov/92514276.

3   Herbert C. W. Goltz, "Michikinakoua," *Dictionary of Canadian Biography*, vol. 5, 1801–1820. (University of Toronto/Université Laval, 2003).

settlers, because he did not believe they could win against such weaponry and numbers. But instead of conceding, his people divested him of his title and rode off to be slaughtered at the Battle of Fallen Timbers.

Michikinakoua traveled up and down the East Coast, shaking hands.

2.

Herodotus's *Histories* [4] report on myths, traditions, battles, political pranks, and wonders. In a section on India, he describes a type of ant that is smaller than a dog and larger than a fox and spends its life building anthills of gold. In another section, he tells of a suitor, Hippokleides, who lost the contest for his bride because he danced too wildly—his performance culminated in a headstand on a table, complete with kicks and gesticulations. His antics disgusted the bride's father. Herodotus questions his sources, sometimes calling a tale "fantastic," or claiming, "as to who was responsible, I can say no more than I already have." His narrative is peppered with phrases like "the Spartans say" and "the Athenians are said to." There is a degree of honesty in this approach: he admits he doesn't know much and that he is often only repeating what he has heard. In the end, he is a teller of tales, hardly to be trusted.

Did the Scythians really drink blood from the skulls of their slain enemies? Did they wear garments made from softened, sewn-together scalps? In my edition of *The Histories*, a footnote describes skulls found by archeologists that bear evidence of scalping, but Herodotus, writing around 420 BCE, was an embellisher. Scalping is one thing; wiping one's mouth with a patch of skin is another.

4 Herodotus, *The Landmark Herodotus: The Histories*, ed. Robert B. Strassler, trans. Andrea L. Purvis (New York: Anchor Books, 2009).

Either way, scalping was a horror conducted long before Columbus made his famous mistake. Scalping was neither brought to North America by Europeans nor "invented" by Native Americans. Even the word *invented* seems wrong. Was slow-slicing—the practice of cutting a victim repeatedly until he bleeds to death—"invented"? Or the attaching of electrical paraphernalia to a prisoner's genitals? Do we seek to name the "inventor" of scalping as a way to free ourselves of guilt? Or to claim it? (*It was us. Blame us. Let us say that we are sorry.*)

Who would think to cut a cap of skin as proof of one's brutality?

In 2 Maccabees:7, a Catholic and Eastern Orthodox book of the Bible, seven brothers are martyred for refusing to eat pork. They are whipped. Their fingers are cut off. They are burned and bled and dismembered. Their limbs are fried in a pan. The first brother's torture is described: "When they had pulled off the skin of his head with the hair, they asked him, Wilt thou eat, before thou be punished throughout every member of thy body?" But each brother refuses to eat. Each brother is killed for his refusal.

It seems that, for a time, almost everyone in North America was scalping. French, English, American, Native American, Mexican. Europeans fighting with each other and with Indians devised a bounty system for scalps, encouraging the practice. Settlers scalped. Indians scalped. Pastors scalped. Parishioners scalped. During the American Revolutionary War, British officer Henry Hamilton was known to the colonists as the Hair Buyer General, because he allegedly paid so generously for the scalps of colonial Americans. John Lovewell, a well-known scalp hunter, once paraded through the streets of Boston wearing a wig made from the scalps of his Abenaki victims, for which he was paid one thousand pounds.

The Mexican government paid for the scalps of Apaches, identified only by their skin and hair color. Chief Gomez of the Mescaleros began paying for the scalps of Mexicans and Americans in an attempt to balance the market. A band of Kickapoo and Mexican scalp hunters turned on each other, the Mexicans claiming the scalps of the Kickapoo and cashing them in with their government.[5]

No matter what color scalp one held, there was someone who would pay for it.

3.

Heads bleed a lot when they're cut. And they have so many nerves. What nightmares lace the sleep of the scalped? Robert McGee's eyelashes look charred.

I could purchase a print of McGee's scalped profile from Amazon.com for $57.00, a savings of $14.25 over some mysterious market price.[6] But where would one hang it? In the living room, above the fireplace? Certainly not in the bedroom. Maybe it would be the first in a collection of prints documenting the violence of one person against another. Or documents of genocide.

Or McGee's could be the first in a collection of portraits of the strangely head injured. His profile could hang beside a portrait of Phineas Gage, a nineteenth-century railroad foreman who was the victim of accidental lobotomy when an explosion at work sent a tamping iron through his cheek, into his brain, and out the top of his skull.

---

5 "The Scalp Industry." http://xroads.virginia.edu/~hyper/hns/scalpin/oldfolks .html.

6 http://www.amazon.com/Historic-Print-Robert-scalped-photographer/dp /B003HQTIFW.

The tamping iron flew a good distance from Gage, taking with it some of his brain and some of his blood. Gage lost vision in one eye, but his head healed. He learned to live a fairly normal life and drove a stagecoach in Chile for years after the accident. But before the accident Gage was known for his efficiency and capability, and afterward he was unpredictable, capricious, fitful, and profane.[7]

8

Next in the collection might hang the X-rays of a contemporary Chinese man's skull, a four-inch blade lodged within. The man, Li Fuyan, claims he was stabbed in a robbery four years before surgeons removed the blade, which they discovered only after the man complained of serious breathing problems and headaches. The blade was corrupted from its time in his skull, lace-edged and rusty. If it had remained there, would the man's body have continued to work at the blade, nibbling at it like some crashed car at the bottom of a lake, corroding the metal until it was only toothpicksized and the man had long since stopped consuming painkillers and wheezing? It was an alien nesting between nasal passages. It was exaggerated shrapnel.

7   Steve Twomy, "Phineas Gage: Neuroscience's Most Famous Patient," *Smithsonian Magazine*, January 2010.

8   Daguerrotype portrait of Phineas Gage. Originally from the collection of Jack and Beverly Wilgus, and now in the Warren Anatomical Museum, Harvard Medical School.

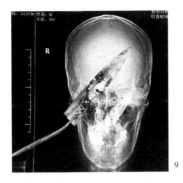

9

4.

In Massachusetts, 1697, young wife and mother Hannah Dustin was taken from her home by a group of Micmac warriors. As the story goes, they marched her barefoot through the snow in her nightgown until they reached their village, where they left her. Her guards, a family, slept beside her, but Dustin stayed awake. She killed the sleepers with a tomahawk and escaped downriver in a canoe with two other abductees. But before they left, they hacked holes in the other canoes so they would not be pursued. Before they left, Hannah Dustin removed the scalps of her ten victims.

Back home, she was paid generously for the two adult male scalps. The rest of the scalps belonged to women and children and so they were worth little-to-no money. A sculpture of Hannah Dustin stands on a pedestal in Boscawen, New Hampshire. Her carved hair and nightgown blow behind her. In one hand she holds a tomahawk; in the other, a bouquet of dangling scalps.

9   "A doctor holds up the knife taken out of Li Fu's brain in China after being lodged there for four year" (AP). Belfast Telegraph, February 18, 2011, http://www.belfasttelegraph.co.uk/breakingnews/offbeat/knife-inside-head-for-four-years-28590542.html.

5.

For many tribes, wearing one's hair in a scalp-lock was not only a matter of honor, it was expected. As described by Ben Armstrong—a white southerner who moved north, learned the Ojibwe language and culture, and was initiated into the tribe in the 1830s—the Indian scalp-lock was a section of hair about the size of a silver dollar, braided at the center of the scalp. The braid was tied off at about half its length, then wrapped tightly in bark or leather, or later, in red flannel—the top choice wrapping because it was flamboyant. The scalp-lock was a trophy a Sioux or Chippewa man was equally prepared to give or take.[10]

In contrast, many white settlers cut their hair as closely as possible, an act that made it more difficult to remove their scalps (the lock allowed for leverage and grip when the scalp was yanked off. Apparently its moment of release was accompanied by a flopping sound). Short hair also made their scalps less desirable trophies.

Does the texture of one scalp differ much from the texture of another? This one stretched and rubbed smooth. This one thick-skinned. This one thin. And how did one treat a scalp in order to keep it supple, to use it to dab the corners of one's mouth? What has happened to all those scalps? The heaps and heaps of scalps that were taken, so many shades of skin, so many colors of hair. Where are they? How long does a scalp last?

6.

General George Armstrong Custer was known for his long blond ringlets. He often posed with guns, wearing a uniform and tall boots. He was a sloucher with a weasel-like face and a moustache like a

10   Benjamin G. Armstrong and Thomas Wentworth, *Early Life Among the Indians: Reminiscences from the Life of Benjamin G. Armstrong* (Ashland, WI: A. W. Bowron, 1892.)

small animal crouching on his upper lip. Among other nicknames, he was *Hi-es-tzie*, Long Hair.

I cannot look at an image of General George Armstrong Custer without imagining bodies strewn across the plains. Four centuries of bodies, brown bodies and white bodies, heaped in ditches and mass graves. Shot. Stabbed. Scalped. Bludgeoned. Is it unfair to see all these in Custer? To try to contain them there?

It is said that Custer polished and smoothed his ringlets with cinnamon-scented oil. All that hair hanging around his chinless face. Would I be more compassionate—more haunted—if he were more attractive? Custer reflects my selfishness, my vanity, my desire for a simple equation: for evil to be ugly.

The history of the Battle of Little Bighorn is one Herodotus would have loved, full of contradictory accounts and unanswered questions. Various people claimed to have dealt Custer his final blow, to have fired the shot that pierced his breast or blew out his brains. When his body was found, there were two holes in it: one through his chest and one through his cheek. It is said that the Lakota left his scalp—balding, the blond locks recently trimmed short—intact. That no one wanted that hair—a valuable trophy, but dirtier than it was worth. Bad medicine, Custer.

Custer died when:[11]

1. Early in the battle, Joseph White Crow Bull, an Ogallala Sioux, shot a rider who wore buckskin and a large hat. The man shouted orders to the troops, indicating he was an officer. But this remembered shot was fired nearly a mile from the place where Custer's body was found. (And who

11 Evan S. Connell, *Son of the Morning Star* (San Francisco: North Point Press, 1984), 389–412.

remembers where they fired a particular shot during a battle? And many riders wore buckskin and hats. Many riders from both sides were killed by friends and allies in the chaos.)

2. Buffalo Calf Road Woman, who fought with the men, knocked him from his horse. His fall was fatal. Or at least final.[12]

3. After years of denying responsibility, claiming that there was far too much smoke and dust during the battle for anyone to know who killed Custer, Rain-in-the-Face, an Unkpapa Sioux, confessed on his deathbed: "Yes, I killed him. I was so close to him that the powder from my gun blackened his face."

4. A Cheyenne named Hawk, who looked similar to Rain-in-the-Face on the day of the battle—both wore yellow body paint, but Hawk carried a larger blue shield—fired the fatal shot.

5. Gravely wounded, his men dead around him, he walked the battlefield alone, then put his own gun to his temple and finished the job.

6. Other.

Custer may have fathered a child with a woman named *Me-o-tzi,* or Monaseetah, "The young grass that shoots in the spring." But the father of her child may have been Custer's brother Tom. It's rumored that the general may have been sterile after a fierce bout of gonorrhea he acquired while at West Point.

---

12   Martin J. Kidston, "Northern Cheyenne Break Vow of Silence." *Helena Independent Record,* June 27, 2005.

Tom Custer was also killed at the Battle of Little Bighorn, his heart carved out of his chest and paraded around on a stick while the Lakota danced and stomped.

General George Custer may have loved a Cheyenne woman. Or, rather, a Cheyenne woman may have been his lover. But her father, Chief Little Rock, had been killed in a battle with Custer's men. And because both George and Tom may have slept with Monaseetah after they killed her father, "love" and "lover" don't seem the right words. Hers was an oral tradition. Things were not written down. Monaseetah, it is said, stayed in her tent. She had a son with a streak of pale hair. She never married. Or she was divorced and notoriously picky. Or, much later, after Custer's death, she married a white man named Isaac. Her name is everywhere in writing about Custer, but there is little agreement in the stories. Custer wrote a letter to his wife—he wrote so many letters to his wife—in which he described Monaseetah's silken hair, waist-long and black as a raven.[13]

It is said that when General Custer's body lay on the battlefield among the dead, two relatives of Monaseetah found him.[14] They called him their relative, persuading the man who was prepared to desecrate his body to leave him alone. Then they thrust their sewing awls into his ears that he might hear more clearly in the afterlife. Clear out the wax. Rearrange his brain.

If, in the case of Phineas Gage, an efficient, kind man turned sour, crass, and volatile after his brain was punctured, perhaps Custer's personality—a whore for the media? A politician? A soldier well acquainted with killing. A murderer—would turn gentle in the afterlife.

13   Connell, *Son of the Morning Star*, 200–202.

14   Connell, *Son of the Morning Star*, 422.

Many reports on the condition of Custer's corpse agree that he looked peaceful in death. That he was sitting upright between two of his soldiers, almost a smile on his lips. That his body was nude but for socks. That it was unmarked and whole. But there are also rumors of his slashed thighs and missing fingers, of arrows through his genitals, and gun smoke that smeared his face. Rumors that those who found him made a pact to spread peaceful falsehoods for the sake of Mrs. Custer. They would say the general's body had not been touched.

But back in 1876, as her husband rode off to his final battle, Elizabeth "Libby" Custer wrote that she was filled with trepidation.[15] Did she dream of her husband's pale scalp flying from a pole, his long yellow hair streaming like ribbons in the wind?

And in another place, not far away, Sitting Bull had a vision of earless white warriors falling on his camp like a swarm of ugly locusts—greasy, crushable, and overwhelming.[16]

15   Elizabeth B. Custer, *Boots and Saddles; or, Life in Dakota with General Custer* (1885, repr; Norman: University of Oklahoma Press), 1961, 220.

16   Jeffry D. Wert, *Custer: The Controversial Life of George Armstrong Custer.* (New York: Simon and Schuster, 1996). 332.

THE DISTANCE BETWEEN IS AN UNBROKEN LINE

The line breaks and separates from itself.
—Johanna Drucker

www.mapmyrun.com tells me that the distance from my house to the building of Languages and Communication (LNCO) at the University of Utah is 1.11 miles. The weather widget on my computer screen tells me it is 27° F and cloudy. Today's predicted high is 39° F. Out my window I can see that it is partly cloudy and that the streets are dry, although the yards are still covered with snow.

The distance between my house and LNCO is slightly longer than the length of yarn it takes to knit a child's sweater.[1]

In my backpack, I have five skeins of turquoise yarn (Red Heart brand, 100% acrylic, medium, worsted), two extra pens, my phone, my keys. In my jacket pocket, I carry a small ball of "natural"[2] merino yarn left over from knitting a pair of fingerless gloves last winter. (The resulting gloves look like therapeutic bandages or casts. Suspiciously medical.)

1 The yarn wrapper informs me that "Every child needs a sweater knit with love." (I have no children. Perhaps I am the end of my family line.)

2 Undyed. In this case, the shorn sheep were cream-colored. The color of a sheep's wool is genetically determined. White is the dominant gene, and black wins out over brown. In Genesis, cunning Jacob strikes a deal with Laban, his father-in-law. Jacob shepherds Laban's flocks, but after years of this work, he's ready to move on. *Don't pay me,* he says to Laban. *Not with money. Just let me keep any brindled or spotted sheep, and you will keep the white ones.* He then selectively breeds the flock, separating the all-white animals from the spotted ones, letting the spotted ones find each other. He builds himself a rapid fortune.

The plan: walk the usual route from my house to the Languages and Communication building on the campus of the University of Utah, trailing behind me a line of turquoise yarn, which will become a map of my walk.[3] I will tie bits of merino to the main line at landmarks, encounters with other people, occasional thoughts, etc. These flag-knots will correspond with the notes I will take while walking, which I will later attach to the yarn in the appropriate order at the corresponding distances. A cartographic walk.[4]

3   A map of my mind. Thoughts all in a line.

4   While Odysseus was away, Penelope sat at her loom weaving a burial shroud for Laertes, Odysseus's father. Odysseus was gone for twenty years. It seemed he was probably dead. *When the shroud is complete, I will marry again,* Penelope told her hopeful suitors. Each day she wove; each night she undid her work. The suitors waited. Some burial shroud! Twenty years of work! While Penelope wove, Odysseus traced an aimless line around the Aegean.

I am fortified with:

3 whole grain pancakes

1 egg (over easy)

1 Mineola orange (surprisingly seedless. Genetically modified?)

3 cups of black coffee

(Such sadness for vegans: no butter. So pleased I am not vegan.)

What if someone or something cuts the line? What if I run out of yarn?

Maybe I will shape the resulting yarn ball like a brain.[5]

It is 10:20 am on Sunday, February 27, 2011. Traffic on South Temple is light, as usual on Sunday mornings.

---

5   *Women must write through their bodies,* writes Hélène Cixous. *Censor the body and you censor breath and speech at the same time. Write yourself. Your body must be heard.* But what does it mean to "write through your body"? I walk. I breathe. I write "coffee" and "oranges." I'll string this yarn along the sidewalk. A pathway. A barrier. Step over it. Duck under it. Follow it to the end. This blue line from here to there. I will be the weaver and the traveler.

Tie[6] yarn to bus stop railing at 1001 E. South Temple. Begin walking. Discovery: I will have to walk backward to unreel the skein smoothly. Discovery: I need scissors. I leave the yarn alone on the sidewalk and go back inside for scissors.[7] Resuming my walk I recognize a surprising degree of self-consciousness. First encounter: a dog-walking couple. They turn around before allowing our paths to intersect. (Avoidance?) I recognize the woman from the bus (Monday and Wednesday mornings, 8:18, Route 6 to the university. Snowy days only.)[8] The harp shop. I have figured out how to walk forward and still unreel: P Street and South Temple. P ST pressed into the sidewalk on each side of the intersection. I think PoST. Then PaST. Then PeST. Heaven Cupcake Truck: Strawberry Chocolate. Lemon Zest. (We Take Credit Cards!) I first saw the cupcake truck in a blizzard, heaped with snow, and thought it had broken down there, stranded and full of unsold cakes, freezing, or growing soft fur. But it has been parked there for at least two months now. I guess the owners live here, and the truck doesn't drive around much during the winter. The giant house where they have fancy looking parties on Friday or Thursday nights. Like Clue. A Murder Mystery. Yellow-lit glam. Q Street. Q ST. QueST. QueSTion. Is QuiST a word? Rebecca's house. I hear she has been sick. R ST. RoaST. ReST. RuST. The pedestrian tunnel beneath South Temple, between the elementary school and its playground, is locked, which means my yarn and I will have to cross at U Street, above ground. END OF FIRST SKEIN. * A tangle. A couple

6   The walk begins. From here, the body of the text (annotations to the walk) will be attached to the line and rolled, note by note, into the resulting yarn ball. Sights, sites, thoughts, encounters, strung and furled.

7   Footnotes break the line. Walking forces the thoughts along. A sentence fragment is an incomplete line, but I'm stringing these sentences together like fish.

8   Dry days I walk or bike.

walks by, says nothing. But then, my back is turned to them and I am crouched on the sidewalk knotting and scribbling in my notebook. I feel vaguely nervous. People don't tend to like unrecognizable acts. Who knows what I might be plotting? The handprints of Michaela and Sean, pressed into the concrete in '95. This project would not be possible in a busier city or a place with more pedestrian traffic. It may not be possible here later in the season, or even later in the day.[9] On another day, the landmarks may remain the same, but the topography of my brain would change. S Street. S ST. SiSTers.[10] LOOK LEFT & RIGHT WHEN CROSSING. FOR ADDED VISIBILITY CARRY ORANGE FLAG ACROSS WITH YOU. (There are no orange flags.[11] Blown away or stolen, waved all along the street, discarded in some yard, some ditch.) A nicely dressed man—tie, black slacks, lavender shirt—pulls a suitcase past without pause. His shirt is untucked. I get out of the way for him. I turn and watch him walking. He pulls out his cell phone. *If you see something, say something.* Windchimes. Yarn like kite string. T Street. T ST. ToaST. TwiST. TerroriST.[12] I think about man Y. His upward curling eyelashes. Geraniums in a window. Blowing Snow. Anticipation of crossing South Temple. Will the yarn make it? Will it be marked by tires? Will

---

9   Or it would be different. The yarn broken more often. More people to talk to. Slower progress. More self-consciousness.

10   I have two: an older and a younger. The youngest is a video artist. Married. Growing a garden. The oldest is the black sheep. Engaged in Miami. *You're all a bunch of hippies,* she says. After Thanksgiving dinner, she turns on the television to watch the football game.

11   In the middle of the night, suffering from insomnia (the days and nights an unbroken line), I have seen a worker in an orange vest adding new flags to the intersections, distributing them like bouquets.

12   Too many letters to fit between the T and the ST, and chalk is too clumsy, but they might fit if written with the finer tip of a Sharpie.

it tangle on someone's car? U Street. U ST. One of the toUgheST. UlSTer is a place in England, right?[13] Crossing South Temple. Watch cars run over the line. Reservoir Park, where there is no longer a reservoir.[14] This park becomes that other park, the small park in Seattle, where I saw a couple walking (a June evening, twilight) and I recognized I was lonely, despite that I was living with man X. How I became like Rapunzel in his apartment, playing guitar for twenty minutes a day,[15] the steel strings building calluses on my fingertips. I repeated after the speaker: ***Buenos días, señor. Buenos días, señor.*** First serious snarl. Hands freezing while I try to untangle. Drop my notebook in the snow. Blue yarn on white snow=*!*!*!*[16] END OF SECOND SKEIN. * It takes four skeins to make a sweater for a small child.[17] Large tree. Swing sets. Sled tracks. Cross University Street. Xeriscape yard: yucca, prickly pear, sagebrush. On a bicycle, or in a hurry, this hill is a bitch. I know where the yarn is behind me. I can see its line, running along the sidewalk downhill, around the curve. Am I still tied to the bus stop out front of my house?[18] I know the

13   A province in Northern Ireland.

14   It's been filled with dirt and turned into a level playing field, but when it rains or snows, the field turns swampy with mud. And although this is a city (such a small one), in winter deer wander down from the mountains to graze here, leaving behind their tracks and droppings. I have seen them running together all along South Temple.

15   I tried to structure my time with routines, a self-imposed schedule.

16   Vivid.

17   If I knit scarves from the resulting yarn ball, who would wear the segments of my walk? How many scarves could I make? Of what length and width? All knit, no perls, for consistency of stitches, for continuity of the lines. A scarf like a block of text.

18   When I wrote letters to friends, I imagined my words as filaments like spider silk, extending from my fingertips across great distances, stringing me to Togo and Italy, San Diego and St. Louis.

line the yarn makes, but I cannot see the line until it is behind me.[19] No dogs have barked at me. No one has spoken to me. Dripping sound of snowmelt. Smell of cigarette smoke. House with beautiful, strange mortar work. Haphazard bricks painted gray. Hidden by tree branches (larch?). The weird surfacing of images is like gasping out of a lake: people used to practice tai chi beneath the West Seattle bridge. I rode past on my bike, where the paste paper wolf[20] was stuck to the pillar somewhere between the recycling stacks and the shipping containers. The traffic lights were long. Snips of white yarn on the sidewalk look like a small heap of pasta. Third skein now the size of a penis gripped loosely in my hand.[21] Flaccid. Crossing 100 South. On campus. END OF THIRD SKEIN. * Stairs by the South Physics Observatory. The yarn takes shortcuts by pulling taut against obstacles. By cutting my corners. By refusing straightness and hard angles. Because I am walking more slowly than usual I detour to a concrete keva, where there are tables with umbrellas and the glass shape of a skylight rises vertically from the ground in a column, like a giant crystal. Through it I can see down into the building below: a table with work spread across it. Some kind of library? And behind

19   But I can't see who intersects with it, or when, or how it shortens its own path as I continue, pulling it taut.

20   I looked for it all over the city—the wheatpasted wolf with long legs, its head turned to three-quarter view, watching. Its best hideout was in the shade beneath the bridge, in the forest of concrete pillars.

21   When Ariadne fell in love with Theseus, she gave him a ball of thread and a sword to carry into the labyrinth, where he would face the Minotaur. *Let the yarn unwind behind you, so you will know from where you came.* He promised that if he killed the minotaur, her half brother, and found his way out of the labyrinth, he would take her with him back to Athens. The Minotaur was sleeping when Theseus reached it, but it awoke for the fight. Theseus killed it and followed the thread back to Ariadne. He took her and her sister to his ship in the harbor, but at dawn he left them sleeping on the beach and sailed away, unfurling his old black sails.

me, on the roof of the South Physics Observatory, is a dome that would open to see the sky. An *oculus*.[22] BUILDING AIR INTAKE. NO SMOKING. Pigeons winging. Fans. I encounter a dog. A boxer. Its owner apologizes for its bark. She leashes it. Maybe the dog is the only one honest and curious enough to admit it thinks I am weird and behaving suspiciously. Icicles on the railing of the Student Services building: Counseling Center,[23] Financial Aid, Registrar. I have cried too much on the balcony level of this building.[24] Part of Laura Veirs "Spelunking,"[25] a song I have been learning on guitar: *(Capo 7. A minor) A large part of me//(D) Is always and forever tied// (G) To the lamplight.* END OF FOURTH SKEIN. * I have walked the distance of a child's sweater. Student Union: I have to pee. Campus is very empty today. Clouds on the mountains behind campus: snaggy and sunlit. Have to cut and retie yarn due to a tangle. Encounter a curious brown Chihuahua.[26] Its owner, a woman, asks what I'm

22   A small dome opens to let a telescope look into the sky. I've never been there but would like to draw my own constellations, draw my own lines between stars.

23   Where I learned to practice various modes of meditation, including walking in labyrinths. You cannot make a wrong turn in a meditation labyrinth. All steps lead to the center and then back out the on other side.

24   After therapy sessions, I tried to collect myself in private before leaving the building. It isn't acceptable to cry in public, to walk around tearstained and weepy. It makes people so uncomfortable. When one doesn't care, crying might be called a subversive act.

25   Don Quixote was lowered into the Cave of Montesinos where he fell asleep and dreamt a world of adventures and he saw his true love. He emerged from the cave like a swimmer, shaking off the underwater world, like a reader who has finally closed her book. Like a footnote, a cave is a pocket, an underworld, a digression from the line.

26   Dogs get away with things people can't, but they're also a point of connection between people; they break personal space, open up little gaps through which conversation enters.

doing. "A project," I say. "For school?" "Yes."[27] She says she likes the color of yarn and I thank her, as if I had dyed the yarn myself? Is she complimenting my taste? Serious yarn entanglement. But I am so close to the end point. I cut and retie the yarn a number of times. Somehow running smoothly again. NO MOTOR VEHICLES BEYOND THIS POINT. Again, the skein grows limp and hollow in my hand. LNCO: I have to try three doors until I find one that is unlocked. I leave the remaining skein collapsed outside the bathroom on the first floor of the LNCO. On the way out I cut the yarn. I will go no farther.

27   I am not forthcoming.

The winding begins. The return. It is very slow progress. I'm on my way out of the labyrinth, but the yarn ball grows too large in my hands, a growing mass of overlapping strands. I am building the labyrinth as I return, taking it with me, the coiled line of my walk. Theseus couldn't forget the labyrinth either. Maybe it was because he was distracted, or traumatized, that he hoisted the wrong color sails. White meant *I have succeeded. I am coming home.* Black meant *Theseus is dead.* At home, his father looked out across the surface of the sea and saw the black sails blowing toward him. Grief-stricken, he leapt to his death. The labyrinth is heavy. The yarn ball gets very difficult to handle. I may have to roll it on the ground as if I am making a snowman. Near the oculus, I watch a runner pause where his path intersects the line, ahead of me. He leans over, breaks the strand, then continues on his way. This solves the problem of the yarn ball being too large to handle. I put the first ball in my backpack and begin winding a new ball. The yarn is broken in five more places, at each busy intersection: at 100 S. and Butler Avenue Butler and University, South Temple and U Street, at T Street, and at P Street. I wonder if it is broken by the force of too many tires driving over it, or if it tangled in a tire and snapped. If it was pulled taut across the street and someone got out of their car and broke it. If someone waiting for a bus found it dangerous, or just irresistible, and broke it. I wonder how long my line has been broken. How long I have been disconnected from that bus stop railing outside my home. How long I have been disconnected. At each break, I am able to resume the line on the other side of the street. A group of people (three) wait anxiously for me between Q Street and R Street. *We're dying to know what you're doing.* I fear that my answer is a tremendous disappointment to them. A runner sidles up to me and we talk about my project as I reel and he wipes his nose. He asks if I have cats (I have one). He says he hopes I do not get carpal tunnel syndrome. Another woman passes and asks if I am knitting. Sort of, I say. The yarn is broken again at P Street, one block from my starting point, but the final block of yarn is gone.

AS A BITCH PACES ROUND HER TENDER WHELPS, SO GROWLS [MY] HEART [1]

Querido,

Our possible love is like the harvest season in a small western city, where people grow produce in their yards. And in this city, I don't have a yard. I live in a second-floor apartment, with only a box of flowers on the sill. Sometimes I steal from other people's gardens.

(The gleaning tally: three peaches, one cluster of very sweet grapes, one Italian plum that tasted like omg-the-most-perfect-sun-sugar-evah [must go back to that tree today!], two strawberries, one cherry tomato, and a little bag full of goodies from Esther's garden—these given freely.)

And so it is with our possible love: covert and delicious, but never mine. It never really belongs to me.

Yours in innocent thievery,

s.

1 Homer, *The Odyssey,* XX.14.

Tenderfoot,

I would get a tattoo if tattoos had the power of metaphor. The way a metaphor results in metamorphosis: the moment it is spoken, the girl that laughs like a hyena becomes a hyena, running across the Sahara, loping and hysterical. I would ask an artist to drive those tiny inkstains into my skin. A seahorse on each ankle would be my wing-fins, my *talaria*, my swift golden sandals. I would be an aquatic Mercury—triumphant messenger—but swimming like a pufferfish in the Super Mario Brothers water levels. Adrift in carnival music, blowing bubbles.

As of yet un-inked,

s.

Fluid Dram,

(I ask you: be mine. But while you are thinking about it, listen.)

The Halloween costume brainstorm is upon me. It is my favorite part of the holiday. Oh!—the tumult of ideas, the tempest, the options for barroom banter. I'd go out drinking every night for this: the possible metamorphoses! I favor a kinetic costume, engineered or interactive, although last year my detonating device failed, and I was forced to be a permanently detonated mushroom cloud for lack of engineering skill. (I built a cloud of Mylar balloons, turned inside out. They were meant to inflate on demand, at the prompting of a CO_2 cartridge and a bike pump, but the balloons were not sealed well enough and the cartridges were too small.)

The first round of ideas includes a collage of the Odyssey (rosy fingers, a sheep skin on my back, a fast black ship jutting from my heart, a golden tapestry hanging from a loom, finger puppets . . .). Or a forest fire (tiny green-leafed trees like a pelt. The pull of some lever and they'll lie down, silk flames will flutter, and the blackened trees will stand. Something like a pop-up book. Like a dog with hackles.). Or Pinocchio with a growable nose would be fun—a nose that ratchets on a crank. I may have convinced a friend she should be not a cloud, but a storm cloud with a rain option (ribbons and glitter?) and a sun option, and a bolt of lightning that ejects from her cloud. But she and I also considered going as a pot roast (her) and baked Alaska (me; "flammable," of course), which quickly led to one of us being an entire meal on a plate (add asparagus and roasted potatoes), and that led to the TV dinner with glued-on kernels of corn. What will you be?

In keeping with my own predictable patterns, Sugarplum, let me compare myself to a mushroom cloud. Or rather, to a person dressed as a mushroom cloud. I was my own metaphor: a precious mess of cheap glitter that sticks to the booze-soaked floor. A performance of something deadly, but, truly, a naked being—pink-skinned me. Freckled and wrinkled and aging, but wearing frayed silver and cotton and taped-together Mylar. Me, pretending to be the embodiment of glamorous, whimsical, invisible, scientifically miraculous, deadly poison.

Yours 'til my cells run amok,

S.

Mi Pobre Hormiguita,

When we ate the raspberries in meditation group I, too, thought of sex, but unlike Adam, who was sitting next to me, his stomach growling, I did not mention it during the debriefing. (Debriefing is not a word we would use in meditation group; it being far too martial for such a context. I think our leader calls it "the checking in." Or does he avoid naming it? He only asks about our experience with the raspberry.) So Adam said he thought of sex, the only one bold enough to say so.

So sex, when it is going well, is a mindful act. The way we focus on each sensation as it happens. The way we notice even the tiniest details—*especially* those tiny details. The scar above your lip. The difference between the texture of the skin on your stomach and that on the inside of your elbow. The way, when we first made love, before we got around to the sex part, you narrated everything as it happened: *I am going to kiss the small of your back. Now, I am going to kiss you right here, on the back of your knee. This spot, here, between your fingers, is a very special part of your body.* How your narration was like a guided meditation, though at the time I'd never done one.

Six raspberries in a white napkin on my lap. *Look at the raspberry,* said the meditation leader. *Study the shape of it. Observe the varying colors.* The raspberry had small hairs and a hollow center. One of the six raspberries on my white napkin (now stained with raspberry juice) was smushed. Each berry was in a different stage of ripeness. *Pick up one berry between your fingers . . . Feel the shape of it . . . Let the raspberry rest in your palm . . . Consider its weight . . . Smell the raspberry.* (The raspberry, under my nose, smelled something like paint.) *Put the raspberry in your mouth and feel it on your tongue . . . Eat the raspberry.* I pushed the little fruit around, tasting it with my different tastebuds, thinking that each zone of my tongue could taste a different flavor—sweetness at the tip, sour on the sides. (I learned later that this isn't true. Our tongues are more of a wildflower garden, the different flavor receptors scattered almost evenly. The average human tongue has two thousand to eight thousand tastebuds—a tremendous range. I hope, of course, that I have a number in the upper range—say sixty-five thousand. Eight thousand may be too many, leaving one overwhelmed and with an aversion to flavors too intense. A childish supertaster.)

The seeds of a raspberry are bitter relief. I swallowed the raspberry. I felt it slide down my esophagus. So small and macerated, it traveled farther into my body.

Mindfully,

S.

Cowlicked One,

Here's the plan: I will divide the canvas into calendar segments. Thirty days in five rows of six. Thirty boxes in a grid. And each day I will chew my food, mash it to a paste between my teeth, my tongue, the roof of my mouth. I will not swallow that first bite but let it fall—nay—spit it onto the canvas. I will press it with my tongue to its corresponding box. A good solid lick.

Box one is stained with raspberry. Box two with kale. Box three with olives—oily. Box four: chickpeas with cilantro and onion and lime. The pastes will harden. Some of them may grow a fur of mold. We will see what happens. I will label them in a Cy Twombly script with the type of food and the date. In pencil.

My last love was like this. Dare I say all love is so? Like food, the first bite so delicious, and we devour it, and soon we no longer taste the flavors, our palate becoming so accustomed. And even the most perfect balance of flavors rots if left on the counter, or stored in the back of the fridge. Day after day, the nutrients go rancid. But then they become texture. They become color.

Sincerely,

The Macerator

Barefoot One,

In summer, the romance of the scholarly life falls away, stripped like finish from wood, and what remains is the bare, splintered, aged plank that might snag my finger, or the bottom of my sock, or might be used like a pumice to smooth the callous on the side of my pinky toe. Once, the scholarly life glimmered like sunshine through leaves in the fall, the leaves not yet turned yellow, but now I sit at my desk writing or reading, and I am not happy in the way that I thought this life of scholarship would make me happy. It no longer glimmers like that. I do not, any longer, feel connected (like a potato, like one aspen shoot to its grove) to all the scholars that came before me. All those who also lived "a life of the mind" at their typewriters, surrounded by stacks of books and papers filled with scribbled thoughts. They drank coffee all night. But in summer I see that it is just me, with my acne and my thinning hair and age-spotted hands, and the unswept floor and the garbage stinking in the kitchen because last night I ate chicken and threw the Styrofoam package and the plastic wrap in the trash can, and I haven't yet bothered to take out the trash. Just me, alone here and growing older—no matter, no matter—and the library books are overdue.

Yours when the snow falls,

S.

Summer Fruit,

Sundrunk, like the bee drowsy from feeding on the pear that fell to the grass, so am I in your presence. But September is blurring into October and the pear is mashed into the grass, all pulpy and fermenting, and its golden-brown skin is withering in honey-mush, half in shadow, under the tree whose branches rise like a candelabra. To the leaves cling spiderwebs, only visible when the light hits them. Tender strands that stitch the pear branches to the sky.

In bloom and in rot,

s.

My Dear Festering Splinter,

The thing is, every metaphor falls apart when you look at it closely enough. The laughing girl is much less like a hyena than she is like a hyena. Beginning with her laugh, the whole reason for the comparison: it is more controlled and lower and less barking than that of those crazed dogs. She wears high heels every day. She has no desire to set foot on the African plain. No analogy ever holds for long. The two things being always two things, with different names, different qualities.

You and I? We are not like skin cells, growing next to each other on one body in a possibly malignant mole. We do not pass fluids between our porous cell walls, osmotically. We do not nestle and exchange, nor divide spontaneously and systematically, cloning ourselves.

We are not two homes in a rowhouse, sharing a wall, allowing the scent of curry to pass between us. If you are torn down, and our shared wall is suddenly exposed. (My outer wall was your inner wall. The books are still on the shelf, along with a sugar bowl and an alarm clock. The place where the stairs once climbed is now a stencil of stairs.) No, we are not like that. We are not a rowhouse. We are not a gap-toothed city. We are not a mouth, not teeth, nor, if you choose to leave me, are you a missing tooth.

Yours truly,

A Single Family Home

THE PIGMENT IN THE WALL

1. A healthy red blood cell circulates through the body for approximately a hundred days, but a brain cell lasts a lifetime. The cells that line the inner lens of the eye are formed in utero and remain with us all our lives. Nonetheless, people often say that every cell in the human body is replaced in seven year cycles. Perhaps this inaccurate claim is cobbled together by averaging the lifespans of various types of cells. Fortunately, our cells pass knowledge to each other like a baton in a magical relay, so even for those that live for relatively short times, there's enough institutional knowledge that we don't forget the basics when cells die—how to walk or swallow—or even the non-basics—how I felt when I didn't make the cut for little league softball when I was ten years old. Still, this bit of inaccurate science is often cited when someone says, dismissively, or by way of excuse, "I was a different person back then," as if having new cells proves the change, as if long-living cells could prevent someone from deeply, significantly *changing*—her mind, her style, her beliefs, her friends, her desires, her career, her living space, the things she boasts about, the memories that bring a hot rush of shame.

2. As a young child, I loved dresses and ribbons, but soon enough, I cut off my braids and wore only pants, a classic tomboy. For much of my life I have been a student. For a time, I was a Christian. For many

years, even into college, I was a competitive swimmer. I have worked as a shoe salesperson, a lifeguard, a photographer, a print technician, an ice cream scooper, a kitchen worker, a restaurant server, a barista, a UPS delivery driver, a temporary employee of Amazon.com, a wildland firefighter, an editor, and a writing teacher. I am an American, a traveler, a vagabond. I am a writer and a reader. I am a daughter, a sister, an ex-girlfriend, and a wife. I am not a mother. I am no longer a girl.

3. When I was twenty-two, and just out of college, I visited a museum in Monterchi, Tuscany, and stood before Piero della Francesca's *Madonna del Parto*, the Pregnant Madonna, which hung behind a protective sheet of Plexiglas. The painting is a fresco, meaning the pigment was painted into wet plaster. Originally, it adorned the wall of a country church, where it was completed around the year 1460. An earthquake destroyed that church, but miraculously spared the fresco, and it was removed from the damaged wall and relocated. During WWII, it was sealed behind bricks to protect it from bombing or looting, and there, in the dark, it grew a quiet fur of mildew. Eventually it was uncovered and restored and relocated again to the museum where I saw it. I had seen reproductions of this painting on postcards and in textbooks.

The *Madonna del Parto*'s forehead is high and broad. Her eyes are downcast. Her robe is deep blue. It was painted with a great deal of lapis lazuli—ultramarine—imported from Afghanistan, a fact I learned in art history class in college. One of the Madonna's hands rests on her hip, the manner of a pregnant woman supporting the weight of her growing fetus, countering the pressure on her back. Her other hand parts her ultramarine gown with two long fingers, offering a glimpse of her swollen belly. A pair of painted angels flank her, holding open a painted scarlet curtain that mirrors the gap in her gown.

My boyfriend and I did not view the Madonna as religiously sacred. Rather, seeing the original was an opportunity to try to understand why this painting of the pregnant Virgin, more than the hundreds of other depictions of her, seemed so special. We stood before the painting for a long time, and our silence, our attention, seemed a form of worship.

4. The tempera paint common in classical paintings was made of egg yolk mixed with pigment, but when I look at paintings of saints and angels, of the Virgin in her blue robe, accented with gold leaf and ultramarine and carmine, I don't think about eggs, or that the pigment is mixed with half of the genetic material that could have been a chicken or a duck. I don't think about how, instead of becoming a chicken, those proteins became color on canvas or plaster, nor do I question if becoming paint is more noble than becoming a chicken (and no egg can be both—neither simultaneously nor in stages). An egg can be breakfast, paint, or a chicken.

5. My college art history professor was young, a woman with dark flyaway curls. The class met after lunch, and despite her engaging lectures full of anecdotes, I often grew sleepy looking at the slides in the dim room. To keep myself awake, I sometimes drew in the margins of my notebooks. I doodled simple faces with closed eyes, their long eyelashes burdened by weights hanging from strings. When my professor showed images of flying buttresses—the sturdy architectural supports that brace the walls of the Notre Dame cathedral—I drew tiny, winged buttocks with smiling faces. Still, I sometimes dozed off.

Now a college writing instructor myself, a student will occasionally doze off in my class, too, despite that they are seminars, and small, and I almost never lecture. Sometimes I wake a student up. Other times, I leave them to fight it on their own. Sometimes, the drowsy one will get up and leave the room, something I never would have done when I was in college, although it may have helped me wake up. Leaving the classroom seemed to me disruptive and disrespectful, and these were not labels I wanted, nor did I want to insult my professor. Of course, falling asleep might earn these labels, too, and most certainly did insult her.

6. To see the painting by Piero della Francesca, I rode shotgun in a borrowed car, and my boyfriend drove us along the winding Tuscan roads. Out the window, I saw old mattresses abandoned in the woods. Prostitution is legal in Italy, but brothels are not, and neither is solicitation in a public place, nor pimping of any kind. Prostitutes are called *lucciole*, fireflies, and I thought of the way fireflies call to each other by flashing their lights against the darkness.

One evening, on a train from Florence to Arezzo, I watched transfixed while the lucciole prepared themselves for a night of work. They laced the backs of each other's shirts, applied lipstick and powder and mascara, spritzed themselves with perfume. They knew how to be feminine, how to be sexy. They were professionally sexy women. They knew so much that I did not know. But the mattresses I saw in the woods were striped and stained and soggy, like old newspapers rotting in the matted leaves.

7. The last time I saw my art history professor was at a "blue party," a goodbye party where the host projected blue slides onto the wall of the house next door, and we all wore blue and drank blue drinks.

And there was my professor, dancing in a tight blue dress. I was surprised to see her there, at a party with her students, most of us undergrads. Late in the night, I leaned woozily against a doorframe and watched her lick blue frosting off of the bare back of the guest of honor, the woman we were bidding farewell.

Did I—do I—think it was inappropriate that she was at that party? That she licked frosting off my friend's back? She was so herself with her students. She didn't care about (in)appropriate. She was an excellent teacher, widely a favorite, smart and interesting. There was nothing blue about her. She was carmine. She was orange or gold leaf, flickering and warm.

8. In Italy my boyfriend and I worked in the kitchen of a school where students from Texas, Colorado, and California studied art and architecture. We set tables for students and faculty, carried bowls of steaming pasta and bottles of cheap wine, washed dishes. The women who ran the kitchen, Giuliana and Lidia, were locals, and from them I learned "kitchen Italian" (spoon, platter), though I could not converse with them. Lidia laughed at the way I ate kiwi, scooping the fruit from its skin like pudding from a dish. She taught me to properly slice a tomato by standing behind me and circling my body with her arms. She held my hands, and I held a small, serrated knife. *Gently*, she said, in Italian, and I understood, because together we held the tomato against the cutting board. Together we sawed so carefully through the fruit. From Lidia, I learned that tomatoes must always be cut with a serrated knife, that the teeth are necessary for breaking the skin. I do not remember the Italian words for *gently* or *serrated knife*. She taught me with the tone of her voice and with her hands on mine. I learned through my body.

9. Why did Renaissance painters choose blue for Mary's robes? Why not gold, or red, or green? Ultramarine pigment was made with pulverized lapis lazuli mixed with oil and purified through a complicated straining process. It was incredibly expensive, since lapis lazuli was imported from beyond the sea. But the word *ultramarine* has always seemed to refer to the quality of the color more than to the origins of the pigment. (Ultramarine! The ultra blue! The blue of the deepest sea! The infinite blue of sky! The transcendent blue of dawn or twilight!) And so Mary wears blue. It seems backward: because it was costly, blue was holy, instead of its innate holiness making it expensive. (*But what is innately holy?*)

10. Blue is a certain speed of light (wavelength interval of 490–450 nanometers). It is a winter night gleaming with constellations, enameled camping cups, and cyanotypes by Anna Atkins—those ghostly outlines of algae, ferns, roots, and petals made by sun and chemicals washed in water. Swimming pools and oceans and the color of barely remembered films, of faded photos, and carnivals on summer nights. Blue(s) is music that growls its way up from the belly and the soul.

11. Like me, my boyfriend was American, but he had lived in Italy for a year or two before we met in Colorado. He had lived with his Italian girlfriend and her family back then. I had seen photos of this ex-girlfriend, and of her sister holding a baby at her hip, and of her mother in a floral housedress burning brush in their backyard. Everything about my boyfriend's past in Italy seemed rustic and romantic to me, but he had returned to the US, which was still home to him. Or maybe he wanted a way out of that relationship, and his Americanness was the way. I never knew. But after he and I had been dating for about six months, he returned to Italy, and I missed him in a way I had not thought possible.

Everything in my life then seemed very uncertain. I was no longer swimming. I was no longer Christian. A friend only a few years older than me had died suddenly. I was about to graduate from college, an English major minoring in photography. There was no pre-plotted professional path laid out for me. I had very little money saved.

In December I graduated and got a job waiting tables. I lived with my parents until I had enough money saved to get to Europe, but before I joined my boyfriend in Italy—our relationship was not certain either, though I was in love with him—I worked for a few months in Ireland. I met a Spanish girl in a youth hostel and together we rented a drafty flat on a street called Nun's Island, wedged between a Catholic School and a river. For money, I served coffee in a café, and I spent my Friday nights baking bread for a woman with a Saturday market stand.

And then I flew to Paris, where the train workers were on strike. I slept on the floor of the train station until I could catch a train out of the city. But there in the train station, I was surrounded by American students who were also sleeping on the floor, waiting for a train. It was early summer, and we Americans were on the loose. I began to panic. In the other Americans, I saw myself, and that I was not unique. I was one of hundreds, one of thousands—young, lucky, loud, and oblivious.

Here I was, working menial jobs while traveling around Europe, able to decide on a whim to travel to Paris or Barcelona or Rome. I could get on any train to anywhere. Anywhere! Around me were all the cities of Europe, all the art in the world, all the travelers I could meet, all the streets on which I could walk, and suddenly the choices became arbitrary. I was paralyzed.

I called my boyfriend and sobbed into the phone. *Just get on the train*, he said. His voice came to me from so far away. *Come to Italy.*

His voice was real, I supposed. He was real, somewhere.

In Italy, he said.

I got on the train and sat on the floor beside an old woman with a bird in a covered cage, and I went to Barcelona where I knew someone, and then, after a couple of days, I got on another train and rode it along the Mediterranean coast (turquoise water, white plaster, laundry flipping in the sun). I knew I was lucky, and I could feel it again.

In Florence my boyfriend met me at the station.

12. Fresco painting doesn't require a binding agent to be mixed with the pigment—no glue or egg yolk—because it is done when the plaster is still damp. Pigments are dissolved in water and applied directly to the wall, so that the painting becomes part of the wall—it is not on the wall, but *in* it. This means that removing a fresco means removing the layers of plaster that contain it. To do this, art restorers press a layer of cheesecloth against the painting and coat it with water-soluble glue. Then they press another gluey layer of cheesecloth against the painting, and so on. Layer after layer of cloth and glue are pressed to the wall. For months, the layers are left to dry, and the cloth binds to the plaster. Then, the surface of the wall is pulled away with all the layers of cloth and glue. The painting and plaster that were once an integral part of the wall are now stuck to the layers of cloth. New plaster is applied to the back of the painting, and it is pressed to a new surface, a new wall. Hot water is poured over the layers of cloth and glue and they begin to peel, one by one, like sunburned skin, until the fresco remains, pressed to its new wall or canvas. This method for removing a fresco is called the *strappo* technique. *Strappo* means "ripping" or "tearing."

13. The Madonna del parto—the pregnant Virgin—is a common subject in Italian Renaissance painting. In such depictions, the Madonna often rests a closed book upon her swollen belly, presumably the Bible, a symbol of the Word Incarnate—Jesus, God made flesh.

In the beginning was the Word.

God said, *Let there be light,* and there was light. God said, *Let there be dry land, let there be oceans,* and there was land and there were oceans. He spoke the animals into being, and he spoke Adam into being, and he tasked Adam with naming the animals. If Adam called a beast *lion,* it was a lion, and if he called it *snake,* it was a snake. Like a writer, the Hebrew God used words to create a world.

14. In Italian *ce* is pronounced like the English *ch,* but the Tuscan accent softens it to *sh.* And so, in Tuscany, my name—Shena—sounds like the word cena, which means dinner.

Pleasure to meet you. My name is dinner.

The Tuscans that I met shook my hand, and repeated my name back to me, with the raised inflection of question: *Cena?*

When I introduced myself, Italians knew that I did not speak the language well, if at all. Perhaps they thought I was funny, or a tease. Perhaps they thought I was stupid. They knew nothing about me, and without skill in their language I could not quickly connect with them. Without language, I was only another young woman with pale skin, brown hair, and a boyfriend who spoke better Italian that she did.

My middle name is Marie, a derivation of Mary, which is my grandmother's name, my mother's name, and my older sister's middle name. A name that connects me to my family, and to the Catholic heritage from which I have distanced myself. I could easily have gone by Maria when I was in Italy, yet another version of Mary, but I had this unarticulated idea that my name and my identity were inseparable, that I had a firm, unique self even in a place where I could not communicate beyond *Where is the bathroom? And I'd like a glass of wine, please.* I thought that my name defined me.

If I had been Maria there, would I have been a different person? Maybe Maria would have been a more confident, more direct person than Shena. Maybe Maria was more Italian, more feminine, less confused. Even now, I wonder at the ways my language creates my sense of self.

15. When I consider the story of Mary, the Holy Virgin Mother, I begin with two possible narratives. In the first, everything is miraculous and true. God impregnates Mary immaculately with the Word Incarnate, and sends an angel to break the unlikely news. This is the religious version, requiring faith and imagination. It is a version that breaks from recognizable contemporary science, and it is a literary version in which words make things happen. Immaculate conception also seems a terrible and terrifying gift. Who would believe it—a pregnant virgin? Pregnant with God's child, with God's divine being? (Not to mention she suffered the pain of bearing of child without even the small consolation that is the pleasure of sex, though in this, sadly, Mary is far from alone.)

In a second version, the scientific one, or the one that I reason through clumsily like a syllogism, Mary is necessarily a liar. Either she lies to Joseph, or to everyone else. Either Joseph is the father of her child, or some other man is. And from there, this version splinters into more possibilities:

1. Mary and Joseph, not yet married, are driven by desire and have premarital sex. They lie about the conception in order to remain "good kids."

2. Despite her betrothal to Joseph, Mary loves another man, and with that lover she gets pregnant. She lies to protect the man she loves, or to protect her unborn child, or to protect Joseph from her betrayal. She lies to protect herself.

3. Mary rushes into the arms of a man that is neither Joseph nor a man that she loves, but simply a man whose body she craves. The same set of lies and protections follow. (This seems the most blasphemous, as if I should not write it: Holy Mary as a lusty woman. We equate love with the sacred, but never lust. Never lust.)

4. Mary was raped. In shame and fear, she lies.

In these none of these versions is Mary a virgin, but if one believes in God, she could still be the Divine Mother. After all, in this story God still takes human shape as Jesus, grows in a woman's uterus, squeezes his way through the birth canal, and emerges as a bloody and gasping human baby that will eventually die a gasping and bloody human death. Why not have a human father too?

16. I try to resist binaries. I try to remember and recognize the ways they limit us. Purity and lust are not sides of a binary. Neither are virgin, whore, mother, holy, crone, girl, innocent. As far as I can determine, there is no specific English word for a person who is no longer a virgin. A woman may not call herself (be) a mother just because she birthed a child, and a woman who has never birthed a child can certainly be a mother.

But can a woman be a virgin and not a virgin simultaneously? Every woman who is no longer a virgin was once a virgin. Every virgin is also not-a-virgin in some other time, whether or not she ever lives within that time. Is potential energy the same as expressed energy? Is this a question for philosophy or physics? (*Another false binary.*)

Regardless of the label on my body now, my mind moves easily between states and times. Still, remembering doesn't make me again what I once was. A virgin is a person who has never engaged in sexual intercourse, but that definition begs other definitions (*What is sexual intercourse?*) These lines are not as neat as language pretends they are. Language is not as neat as we pretend it is, though it is very powerful.

17. When I washed dishes at the school, I wore a rubber apron. I loved the invincibility it provided, the weight and smoothness of it. It was the costume of a Worker. It felt like something one might wear for work dirtier than dishwashing: to shovel slag, or rinse the blood from the floor of a slaughterhouse.

Lidia and Giuliana did not work on weekends. Instead, on Saturdays, one of us kitchen staff would slice bread and fruit and set out Nutella and butter and jam, and the students would filter through the dining room whenever they felt like it. We made them cappuccinos or espressos or lattes, and then we washed the dishes and the kitchen floor. When it was my Saturday to work, I always turned up the volume on Bruce Springsteen's album *Born in the USA*, and I washed the floors wearing the rubber apron, dancing with the mop, longing for a motorcycle on some New Jersey road that I had never seen because I have never been to New Jersey. It seemed to me then that Springsteen's music was innately American. That knowing what it felt like to ride a motorcycle in New Jersey was innately American, and that by listening to Springsteen, I knew it. I loved being in Italy, but some small part of loving it was in my homesickness.

18. My boyfriend and I often sat on the courtyard wall and smoked cigarettes. I was not a smoker, but that wall overlooking olive groves and stone streets seemed made for smoking. In Italy, it seemed like

smoking connected me to long-dead Tuscans, to winemakers and olive farmers, to beautiful girls in lace and lipstick. To the art restorers who perched on scaffolding and set down their chisels for a break, dangling their legs over the piazza, shouting hello to their friends that passed below. To the hunchbacked men who sipped espresso and watched soccer in the bars every afternoon. Still, I felt a little sick after every cigarette.

19. Della Francesca's *Madonna del Parto* has a long neck and fair skin. A halo rings her head like a balanced basket. Her hair is held back from her high forehead with elaborate twists of white cloth, making her appear almost bald.

High foreheads were considered beautiful during the Italian Renaissance. They're everywhere in the paintings of Venus, of the Virgin Mother, of Duchess patrons. In della Francesca's painting, the Madonna looks strangely youthful, almost like an infant, tender-cheeked, vulnerable, and bald.

The fingers parting her gown are awkward. They seem to bend strangely, and the hand appears a bit too wide for the fingers, but there is a lightness to her touch despite the awkward forms. And there is something erotic in the gentle parting of that gown, the teasing of the layers beneath.

20. Roland Barthes writes that the eroticism of striptease arises from the barriers of clothing that hide the woman's nakedness. The cigarette holder, the furs, the feathers: these provoke the viewer and enforce the idea that *nakedness* is a woman's natural state. Beneath those layers, she is naked. They also leave something to the imagination, and this is where eroticism dwells and blooms.

We humans wrap ourselves in clothing for protection and for warmth. Even during infancy, we are clothed: in bonnets and booties, in pinks and blues, in our given names, in our expected genders, in the expectations of our families. None of these are innate or natural. And if we grow to inhabit them, it can be difficult to peel them away. When we do, what is left? Who is there? (*Are we more than our accumulated labels?*) But if we do not grow to inhabit them, but discover we have been clothed in the wrong layers, the wrong color, the wrong gender, the wrong name? Some of us, bravely, put on our chosen layers and ask—beg, sometimes—for others to acknowledge them.

21. I cannot remember much about the first two times I had sex with that boyfriend, though they were the first two times in my life. Still, I say two times, because I always discount the first time, trying to erase it, to call it a rehearsal. To name the second time as the first because it is a story I prefer.

The second time, we were staying in a pensione on the Mediterranean coast. Waves crashed against the rocks below. The waves were deep blue, and he was patient, and the sex was awkward and unsatisfying because I didn't know how to move my body with his, against his. But this is the story I tell myself.

There are no rehearsals.

Or every time is rehearsal.

Or every rehearsal is also a performance.

Or everything is rehearsal and performance, [un]mediated, all at once. Performance, rehearsal, unplanned action: all equally [un]real.

22. If you transfer a fresco to a new wall, what becomes of the old wall? Part of it goes with the painting because the painting is the wall.

They are not separate entities. But the rest of the wall, the part with-out the paint, is destroyed or replastered and repainted. The new wall that receives the old painting becomes a collage of times and places.

23. After we looked at the *Madonna del Parto*, we drove the bor-rowed car to the top of the town and looked across another valley full of olives and grapes. My boyfriend set up his 8 x 10 view camera while I took a photo of him with a point-and-shoot. He was perched at a bend in the stone wall, one foot on each side of an angle, the tripod legs balancing with him, the camera lens aimed at the patch-work land. But before he could meter the scene or compose a photo, it began to rain torrentially. He could barely break the camera down before our clothes were stuck to our skin, soaked through and trans-lucent. In the photo I had snapped, the storm was at our backs, and the sky he looks at is pale and bright and all the leaves are glimmer-ing, no sign of the storm that was already upon us.

24. Once upon a time, the plaster in the wall was plain and damp. The fresco was painted and became part of the plaster. By the time the fresco was removed, the pigment had long been inextricable from the plaster. It seemed as if the wall had always held the image.

25. My boyfriend and I did not leave Italy together. I flew first to London to visit a friend who was on leave from the Peace Corps. My friend was stationed in a village in Togo, and when I met him in London he was culture shocked, overwhelmed by the city, and unhappy about his life in Togo (*what was he doing there?*) But after that visit, he returned to the village and completed his second year of service. In that second year in Togo, when he successfully argued a

friend out of jail, he found his calling. The next time I saw him, two or three years later, he was living in Washington, DC, studying international humanitarian law. It was as if the painting had always been in the plaster. But I was waiting tables in restaurant after restaurant, moving from city to city, a vagabond. I left every place. Will I call a place home someday and feel I have always been headed there? Will I know myself completely then? (In asking, I hear these questions as ridiculous.)

26. My boyfriend flew out of Rome a few days after me. His flight was to leave Rome very early in the morning, so when he packed his things back in our sublet apartment he took the alarm clock I had left behind. It was an imitation of an old analog clock, the kind with twin bells on the top, and its ring was startlingly loud. He had always hated that clock, but without it, he would never wake early enough to get to the airport on time, so when he went to sleep that last night in a hotel room in Rome, he set the alarm, and when it woke him in the dark morning, he grabbed it and flung it—still ringing—out the open window. It clattered and broke on the street below.

27. You can break a clock, but time will continue on its course. My boyfriend and I broke up not long after we returned from Italy, but once in time we lived together in that small sublet apartment, with its lofted bed and its skylight, and in the afternoons, the sun came through the skylight and cast a rectangle of light across the white sheets, which were always a little stiff from line drying. Through the course of the day, the rectangle of sun traveled across the bed, a beam of light that made visible and insistent the passage of time.

28. I am writing this in Salt Lake City, near an ancient salty lake that used to fill the entire valley. The city and its oozing suburbs sit between mountains, lake, and river, as if in the bottom of a bowl. I can see the geologic history of this place as strata when I hike in the hills that overlook the city. Well-trod trails circle the mountains like a waterline, but this is a dry place now.

I have lived here for five years, a very long time for me in my adult life. I have lived many places, some of them for only three months, and when I leave here, it will be for an academic job or fellowship where I might live for a single year, or maybe for the rest of my life.

29. It has been fourteen years since I was in Italy, nothing compared to the number of years since Piero della Francesca painted his Madonna del Parto into the damp plaster of a tiny Tuscan church. Still, according to folk wisdom, my cells have cycled through my body twice since then. I am twice a different person.

But this is also a ridiculous notion. Like a fresco painting, I cannot tell where the new plaster merges with the ancient paint. I cannot tell which part of me is a writer, and which calls herself dinner. Which woman holds the cigarette, and which is the child or the photographer or the nude. I study my hand that once held a cigarette while I sat on a wall in Tuscany. It still bears a faint scar where I cut myself whittling when I was a child. My nails are bitten low, but they keep growing. How long before the root becomes the tip that I bite?

Am I the woman who danced with the mop while listening to Springsteen? Am I the one who waited tables in Denver and Washington, DC, and Bowling Green, Kentucky? The one who believed, with something that felt like certainty, in God?

I tell myself sometimes that I have left those women behind, that I have exchanged them, her, for new cells, a new me. That I have sloughed her cells into carpets and sinks, washed them down drains, let them blow across mountaintops and bike trails. I let them drift along roadsides. I left her scattered on faded pillowcases.

But I know, somehow, I hold that woman within me still. I taste her on my tongue as I swallow her down.

A PERFECT TIME TO THINK SILVER

I am not greedy. I do not seek to possess the major portion of your days. I am content if, on those rare occasions whose truth can be stated only by poetry, you will, perhaps, recall an image, even only the aura of my films.
—Maya Deren

1. A BEGINNING

Eleanor said, *Find me a new name*, so he named her Maya—mother of the Buddha. Mother of Hermes. Greek goddess of mountains and fields. Hindu illusion. As for her last name, it had been amputated years ago, back when her father began working with the feeble-minded children of New York.

Maya and Sasha lived on the entire top floor in an old house, with a big south-facing window. There was a teakettle and a hot plate. They drank coffee on the fire escape as if in a treehouse, in a nest of black iron and leaves. The place was filled with indirect light and bamboo furniture. They sat on and slept on and shoved around an array of couches. The fireplace mantle held large bottles of rum. They swept the floor. They read so many books on the couches. When they were filming, crumpled tinfoil accumulated in the corners. They used it as reflectors. They hung sheets of paper, propped mirrors against the walls. Maya often held them—broken or whole—in the films.

Tinfoil, mirrors. There were no plants, no curtains. Sasha held the camera and watched Maya through the lens, her curls and long fingers.

Maya's bedroom was blue and full of seashells. On the ceiling, a painted sea creature glowed in the dark.

2. FILM: *MESHES OF THE AFTERNOON*

Unlock the door. Climb the stairs, past the off-the-hook telephone. From the window, watch the woman in black walk away, down the long path, holding a flower. This is in California, along a cliff. The sea is down there somewhere. The woman turns and her face is a mirror, but she is too far away. You will never catch her, never see your reflection. Flash of the mirror. She turns.

Unlock the door. The record spins. The hand lifts the needle. Replaces the telephone receiver. She turns this way and that. She puts one hand to the glass, then the other. She looks into the distance. Her reflection wears a crown of leaves.

Unlock the door.
The knife, the key, the crooked stairs.
The knife on the table with the bread and the coffee cup.
The key on the tongue.
The key on the open palm.
The painted stairs.
The flower in the bed.

The knife in the bed.
The key in the mouth.
The key on the table.
The hands on the glass.
The woman on the walkway, high above the ocean.
The flower in the hand.
The knife in the hand.
The key in the mouth.
The blood on the throat.
The key in the hand.
The key on the table.
The key in the hand.
The key on the table.
The key in the hand.
The blood on the hand.
The phone off the hook.
The eye and the mirror.

3. MIRRORS

Some say Maya Deren's films demonstrate an obsession with the concept of the alter ego. Mirrors and repeated characters abound, and she often starred in her own films, sometimes playing multiple versions of herself. But she never credited herself as an actress, perhaps inviting the viewer to see her not as a narcissist but as a stand-in for any self, for the psyche, the viewer, the dreamer.

"The girl in the film is not a personal person; she's a personage," Deren said. I am surprised by the quality of her voice. It is not petaltoned, but sharp, with a little rasp, like she's smoked plenty of cigarettes.

Maya's mirrors are evasive, always turning away. One could say that "starring" in her own films was narcissistic, or one could say it was practical. Or one could say she starred in her own films because she knew she was beautiful, and because Sasha knew she was beautiful too. They made the films together.

4. TESTIMONY: STAN BRAKHAGE (THE PHOTOGRAPHER)

"All of Maya's symbolism was very simple. Maya had the capacity to speak more directly about what everyone else was being very pompous about—that is, symbolism, particularly psychological symbolism—than anyone else I ever met. If one underestimates such a talent, then I suggest trying to make a film that uses the obvious psychological symbols like keys and knives as "Meshes" does, and not bring down the house with laughter."

"Maya . . . cut her teeth on such symbols."

5. A KNIFE

A knife is a tool for hunting, skinning, scraping (a hide, for example), butchering, food preparation (slicing, dicing, chopping, mincing, spreading), defending yourself when threatened by animal or human aggressors, harvesting (bananas, wheat), ritual sacrifice (of chickens, goats, bulls, for example, or—if you are the biblical figure of Abraham—your unwitting child, or if you are ancient Mayan, slicing out the heart), mugging, murdering, performing ritual suicide (Japan), forcing another person into action, performing surgery, performing an autopsy, splicing film, jimmying a lock, extinguishing a candle, opening a can or bottle, carving initials or drawings in tree bark, sculpting or whittling, carving a jack-o'-lantern, clearing brush, kudzu, or other thick vegetation, scarification, turning a screw, sharpening a pencil, scratching your back, cleaning your fingernails, picking your teeth, fishing, easing pain in childbirth (superstition [source is dubious]: place knife under bed), protecting a baby from evil spirits (superstition [Chinese]: stab blade into headboard), protecting the dead in the afterlife (superstition [Anglo-Saxon]: place knife in the grave), preventing nightmares (superstition [Greek]: place knife under pillow), cursing (superstition [Anglo, American, widespread]: gift a knife to sever a relationship), stirring strife (proverb).

A knife is useless for: Defending yourself against lightning.

What is a knife without a hand or a table? A floating knife. A symbol of a knife. An icon.

6. UNREELING

Her pockets were full of notes, schedules, and possible shots, but despite the index cards, Maya often kept Sasha waiting. There were many films she did not complete, thousands of feet of cellulose packed away in canisters and coffee cans.

Sasha held the camera while it collected light, frame after frame of Maya's freckles and pale skin.

They were two filmmakers with one film, and so they made another. Maya followed the cat around. The cat pawed open a door, sniffed at a box, birthed a litter of kittens, licked them clean.

This is the way Maya filmed: the camera tracked the psychic landscape. It was Sasha who knew how to show three Mayas sitting together at a table. Maya shoved the camera into a cabinet: a cat's-eye view, looking for a place to give birth. Sasha took the close-up of the cat's eye, the whiskers, the suckling kittens.

No matter.

In the end, or in the middle, Maya took the camera and Sasha took up with her friend.

7. EMPTINESS WILL BE FILLED BY RITUAL

Teatime. Knitting. Hopscotch. Ceremonial dance. Let the man be the maypole around which the women weave their ribbons.

The Wikipedia entry for "emptiness" features a photo of an empty subway stop, a tiled tunnel, lacking its rush hour crowd. "A metaphor," the entry says. This echoing, fluorescently lit chamber can "symbolize the sense of void and isolation that a person may feel" when depressed.

I imagine the depressed person googling "emptiness." Would this image make her laugh? The subway tunnel of the soul? A symbol that will bring down the house with laughter? A disambiguation link leads to an entry for a Chinese constellation named, in translation, "emptiness" that depicts the ruins of a mansion (虛宿).

8. FILM: *RITUAL IN TRANSFIGURED TIME*

1. The widow moves between dark rooms, horizontally, along the axis of time.

2. She whirls a skein. (Some game of cat's cradle.)

3. *Come and play. (She invites her younger self.)*

4. *Is it still time if it is wound into a ball?*

5. *A coil is neither horizontal nor vertical.*

6. *The virgin winds while the widow whirls.*

7. *When the ball is whole it is time.*

8. *The whirler vanishes.*

9. *Or the whirler and the winder are wound together.*

10. *She dances through a party.*

11. *Touch their bodies like a pane.*

12. *No thank you.*

13. *No thank you.*

14. *Games. Such as farmer in the dell.*

15. *Such as blind man's bluff.*

16. *Three graces.*

17. *He lifts and drops her (her ankle buckles).*

18. *Such as farmer in the dell.*

19. *No thank you.*

20. *The grass grows. There is no horizon.*

21. *He is Pygmalion.*

22. *She did not know how to properly pan and so the trees strobe.*

23. *The little hills do leap so the trees do leap.*

24. *(She won't have him) (or death is on her heels).*

25. *Underwater, the world is reversed.*

26. *In negative, her scarf is a veil.*

27. *Even underwater, gravity pulls a body toward the center of the earth.*

28. *The veil is in her mouth.*

9. A GUGGENHEIM

In Haiti, Maya collected eighteen thousand feet of Vodou trance footage: writhing arms, billowing clothes, rolling eyes, white floating wings of chickens. She took a liking to Erzulie Freda, spirit of all you do not need for life: love, beauty, jewelry, dancing, luxury, and flowers.

At the ceremony, when she became a priestess for Erzulie Freda, no one had a camera.

The procession bobbed through the streets. On a man's head was a wide flat box, like a boat, full of sacrificial bits—toy ships, rum, damp towels. More white wings floated and spun. From the street to the shallows, through the reeds into the licking waves into the sea. Then they saw Maya so far out in the ocean, walking. So far out, and the waves swelling. She waved her arms. She became strong.

10. TESTIMONY: STAN BRAKHAGE

Vodou became the dominant force in Maya's life. She was permanently "possessed" by it. Vodou transcended even her filmmaking. Despite thousands of feet of film footage collected on multiple trips to Haiti, she was unable to make a film about Vodou ritual. Instead, she wrote a book.

"She felt that, whatever way she approached it, the result would be too superficial. She did not believe that the film had captured what really was involved in the mystical experience of this religion."

11. INCOMPLETE FILM (now *THE DIVINE HORSEMEN*)

1. Four women walk along a road. On the far side of three black trees, four white dresses blossom. You are too far away to see what the women are carrying.

2. Symbols drawn in the dirt with flour. Vertical is the axis of the universe. Horizontal is the axis of the story. At the crossroads of the universe and the story, the gods enter. Chickens float. Whole bodies made of wings. Whole bodies made of unfolding fans. Whirl the chickens by the legs so they cannot walk away with your sins.

3. A line of plants in jars and bottles. Paint streaks the wooden tabletop. This is a dark room, a dark shot, a pause from spinning chickens with broken legs. A pause from the lifting skirts, the shuffle of bare feet in dirt and flour. (The god likes to dance in bare feet.) This is a pause: Large bottles of rum with very disturbing looking roots in them—the trapped souls of something or other. Twisty and gnarly is the trapped soul.

12. EVEN THE TREES DO LEAP

Back in New York, she forgot her purse in the movie theater. Or it may have been her gloves. When she went back for it, she found the boy, Teiji, sleeping beneath the seats. He was fifteen years old, homeless, an untrained musician. She took him home. After all, she had so many couches.

Teiji Ito was the child of a dancer, slim and smooth-faced. Living with Maya, he began drumming.

And so began the dancing, the chalk, the cats fighting day and night. And no one slept on the many couches anymore because there were drums and flutes and rituals and dances and chalk patterns on the floor, and in some cases, a nude ill person who was being treated for some disease or for possession.

13. TESTIMONY: STAN BRAKHAGE (ON MAYA'S CATS)

"One of the ironies that she loved so much was that the Siamese cat behind the chicken wire, named Erzulie after the Haitian goddess of love, was so desperate a bitch that she fought with everything that came near her. I particularly remember her other cat, named in honor of Ghede, the Haitian god of death and life, as the most enormous cat I ever saw in my life—it was like a small mountain lion. These two cats, Ghede and Erzulie—Death and Love—used to parade back and forth on either side of the chicken wire shrieking the worst feline obscenities at each other."

14. TRANCE

From transir—*to cross over. An intermediate state between sleeping and waking; a half-conscious or half-awake condition; a stunned or dazed state. A state of mental abstraction from external things; absorption, exaltation, rapture, ecstasy.*

Trajectory and suspension. Hanging in the doorway. Walking through an intersection. Moving between human and divine, conscious and subconscious, upper and lower, narrative and footnote.

15. FILM: *MEDITATION ON VIOLENCE*

In China, she learned, that which has the ultimate form has no form. That which is constant motion contains all possible forms. The perfect form exists as long as the beautiful one remains in motion.

The dancer leaps. Skin over ribs. Fluid, then kicking. The blade in the hand. With one jump we are high up and then we have the open sky. The blade jabs and flashes. The shadow leaps and stretches. The camera circles. Maya's shadow dances, too. The hand grips the blade. Kicking, then fluid. Skin over ribs.
Leap, leap.

Leap, leap.
Ribs under skin. Fluid, then kicking. The hand grips the blade. Maya's shadow dances too. The camera circles. The shadow stretches and leaps. The blade flashes and jabs. We have the open sky with one jump and then we are down. The blade in the hand. Kicking, then fluid. Ribs under skin. The dancer leaps.

16. A WEDDING, A TRANCE

Two dancers married. At their wedding reception, Maya, possessed by Papa Loco, was outcast to the kitchen, growling and roaring.

Step shuffle shuffle shuffle fall back. Step hop shuffle shuffle shuffle.

She threw a refrigerator across the room. It hit the opposite wall. She catapulted silverware and china, pots and pans and watermelons.

Yes—*impossible*—but the photographer was there, and he tells us it was so.

The groom took Maya upstairs. He soothed her: *Papa Loco, Papa Loco, Papa Loco.*

Who knows the drumbeats that it took, the shuffle steps and the shaking? She called for the photographer. *Stan!* The groom held him and Maya doused him in liquid—was it rum?—and then in flames.

Burning suit, thought the photographer. *My only suit is burning.* He patted at the flames.

Thank you, said Maya. *Thank you. Thank you.*

The suit flickered blue, but was, in the end, unscathed.

17. THE END

In the end, Maya Deren died of a brain hemorrhage. Malnutrition, it was said, exasperated maybe by Dr. Max Jacobsen's magic brown potion, which she injected often and liberally, into her fanny (fanny: my grandfather's preferred word for butt—he thought it the politest euphemism, though it is so impolite in British English). Dr. Max Jacobsen's magic potion was mostly speed, but Maya thought it was vitamins. She injected it before parties, to *steel herself.* She was tired.

In the end, there was a room full of shelves full of boxes full of reels and reels of cellulose, full of latent dances that have not been seen since they were danced.

In the end, she may have died of anger—there was a fierce battle over her husband's inheritance. For Maya, there was no small anger, no small love.

In the end, she was forty-four years old.

BY SOOT, BY FLOUR, BY BEETLE TRACK

When Navius, expert in augury that he was, immediately said that it would happen, Tarquin replied: "Well, I thought that you would cut a whetstone with a sharp knife. Here, take this and do what your birds have predicted would be possible." And Navius, hardly delaying at all, took the whetstone and cut it.

—Livy, *History of Rome*, 1.35.2

In stars. In flour. In clouds. In palms. In the bend of a myrtle branch. We squint to glimpse the future. We read and misread. We swallow the tea and study the leaves at the bottom of the cup. If the cheese coagulates just so, the marriage will fall apart, but what difference does it make if there is nothing we can do to stop it? And if we foresee it, will we not make it so?

Tyromancy: fortune by cheese, with particular attention paid to coagulation

In the classical world, an augur read the flight patterns of birds. With a curved wand, he divided the sky into quadrants. Not all birds foretold the future, but owls, ravens, woodpeckers, and bearded vultures had the power. Gods spoke through their methods of flight or resting, the pitch and direction of their voices. An eagle trumped a woodpecker if both were present. But since augurs were human, they often ignored or imagined signs, looked in the wrong direction, or chose when to read. No matter how carefully the procedures were delineated, signs often conflicted or turned out to be wrong. The history of bad readers is a long history.

Umbilicomancy: fortune by umbilical cord
If the umbilical cord stretches straight, the baby will live a life of ease, but if it is looped around itself, the child will have a wild imagination. If it is looped around her arm, she will always work for others. Around her neck, she will be a slave to love. If around an ankle, she will wander from place to place. She will never know home.

If I loop the cord before they cut it, can I change her future? If she lives, she will be beautiful.

Skatharomancy: by beetle track
Shuffleromancy: by electronic media player (such as an iPod)
Scapulomancy: by oracle bones

In ancient China, turtle plastrons—the ventral surface of the shell—were heated until they cracked. Females' shells were used more often, maybe because they are less concave. Ox and sheep scapulae were also useful. The cracks revealed crop yield, the future of the royal family, the outcome of a battle. The answer was carved or inked onto the bone. Later, farmers sometimes unearthed the bones and buried them again without noticing the inscriptions. For a time, bones were ground to powder and swallowed to treat malaria and knife wounds. In 1899, Wang Yirong, a collector of Chinese bronzes, fell ill with malaria. Before his friend ground the bones for his treatment,

Wang noticed the writing on them. For years, the Chinese had consumed the foretold futures of their ancestors, but now they began to collect them.

What did the ancient Chinese want to know? Whether misfortune was coming. Whether a particular dead ancestor was causing one's toothache.

Dactylomancy: by finger movements
I argued with a friend about whether or not the relative lengths of our fingers disclosed our sexual orientations. Digit ratio, she said, is visual, cellular proof of biologically determined sexuality. She is partly right: digit ratio is largely determined by the amount of testosterone present during a particular stage of fetal development, and "masculine ratio" in women (the fourth finger is longer than the second finger) often correlates with same sex attraction. Yet this equation is too simple. Just as I cannot know a person's sexual preferences by knowing the shape of her genitals, I cannot know it by the lengths of her fingers.

Urticariaomancy: by itch
Everything depends on the location of the itch.

> Left ankle: marriage or money.
>
> Spine: disappointment.
>
> Nose: You will be kissed or annoyed. Or you will meet a fool within the hour.

Shortly after I met the person I would marry, I developed an itchy rash on my shin (an unpleasant surprise). Soon, it appeared on my elbow (not listed). Then on my thigh (a change of residence). The quarter-sized blotches grew larger and scalier. I slathered myself in calamine and anti-fungal creams. The rash continued to spread. It grew scabby and cracked. The doctor prescribed Cortisol, but it didn't work. The homeopath couldn't help either. My arms swelled until I was unable to bend my elbows. Vaseline, said the doctor. It will at least help with the healing, if not subdue the rash. Prednisone and antihistamines: the swelling subsided, but not the rash. Boot heel scraping shin. The scabs bled. I tried sleeping on the floor— maybe I was allergic to my mattress? The carpet was worse. I kept my fingernails short and filed. Vacuumed. Laundered. Locked the cat out. Slept in a tent in the garden. All night coyotes circled and stars slid slowly across the sky. My strange sleeping habits and the state of my skin strained my relationship. Don't scratch. Don't scratch. Finally, and with no explanation, the rash began to heal. But what did it foretell? It came to pass: I am sometimes difficult to love.

LIGHT IS A WELL-SHOT ARROW

THE NAMING OF THE MOONS

Saturn has eighty-two moons, but in 1847, when John Herschel suggested that Saturn's moons be named after the nine Titans and Titanesses, Saturn's mythical siblings, he only knew about eight of them. He hadn't seen the entire kingdom of circling spheres, including small shepherd moons that travel with flocks of ice and dust, nestled in the gaps of Saturn's rings. He didn't know about the slew of miniscule moonlets. When more than nine moons were discovered, the namers resorted to other Roman gods and mythological figures. Then they named the irregular moons after Inuit gods and Gallic gods, and finally, after the Norse Ice Giants.

A SMUDGE OF ICE

In 1835 Herschel traveled by ship to South Africa in order to study the southern skies. There, he noted, among other things, the return of Halley's Comet. The rhythm of the stars is so much slower than the rhythm of waves, but the same beats wash over us that washed over ancient Babylonians, who marked the appearance of the comet in cuneiform on clay tablets, and over John Herschel as he peered through a telescope somewhere in South Africa in 1835.

Few people see Halley's Comet twice in their lifetime. If a person is a curious, skygazing youngster, born near the comet's presence, and her vision holds out as she ages, she just might see it twice. The comet was last visible in 1986, but it was under the worst viewing conditions recorded during the past two thousand years, the sun positioned between comet and earth. I was ten years old in 1986. It was 4 AM, and like ducklings, my sisters and I followed our dad through crusty snow to a beach on the shore of Lake Michigan. Our toes grew numb inside our boots while our dad studied the place in the sky where we were supposed to see the comet—he was a subscriber to a monthly sky map—but he could not find it. A week later we saw it from our backyard, a smudge in the binoculars like a thumbprint, dusty and pale.

In 2061, when the comet returns, I will be eighty-five years old (if I am lucky—or is this luck? It depends, I suppose, on whether eighty-five means forgetfulness, infantilization, drool, and pain.) But say it's luck, and my eighty-five-year-old self leans into the eyepiece of a telescope and sees Halley's icy trail as it passes us once again. Earthbound, I will marvel, far more than I did at age ten, that a cold, inanimate rock can glow, can move so swiftly through the galaxy, while I, with my ninety-eight-degree blood and the electricity sparking in the mysterious coils of my brain, can move at only two miles per hour.

THE FLOWERING DIVISION
OF THE VEGETABLE KINGDOM

Herschel is credited with the word *photographie*, although it had actually been coined four years earlier by the French Brazilian Hercules Florence. Herschel also used light-sensitive vegetable juices to make "phytotypes" and discovered how to make photographic images permanent by using hyposulphite of soda, what we called "hypo" or "fixer" all those days and nights in college when I stood in the red light of a darkroom, singing along with some minor key pop song, watching chemicals slosh in a tray.

Herschel was friends with the scientist John Children, after whom a python and a mineral are named—the Children Python (a python for kids!) and Childrenite. I imagine Childrenite as a rock that grows a crop of grubby toddlers, but really it's a vitreous, inanimate crystal that looks like dirty quartz, brownish and growing at splintered angles, like the fingernails of Nosferatu.

Herschel was also friends with Children's daughter, Anna Children Atkins, who made famous the cyanotype process, another of Herschel's inventions. The cyanotype is a photogram, a contact sun print made on Prussian blue paper. The object one places on the paper leaves behind a pale silhouette, a negative of its shape.

In college, I once used Prussian blue to print a series of letters to my sister, who was younger than me, but also in college. The letters were handwritten, in cursive script, and included small portraits of my sister. In one, I asked her to play dress-up with a box of diaphanous fabrics that she draped over her shoulders and her head. She held them out against the light that shone through the window. It was winter, and the trees behind her were bare. In another, I asked her to open her mouth wide, to pretend she was shouting, and I focused on the gap between her front teeth, the dark cave of her mouth. I bound the printed letters in twine and tucked them into a handmade envelope.

DAUGHTER OF A SCIENTIST

In the early nineteenth century, women were not encouraged to learn or study science. While men gathered in London to share their findings at the Royal Society, the women walked across the fields, made tea, raised children, ran households. But Anna Atkins's mother died after giving birth to her. Anna was her father's only child. She drew seashells for him. She illustrated his translation of *Genera of Shells* with pencil drawings, quiet coils, like ears.

When I look at her drawings, I want to hold one of those shells in the flat palm of my hand, make it a talisman. I would whisper into its whorls and seams. I would stop biting my nails. I would slip it into my pocket for when I needed it.

Atkins is known for publishing the first book of photographs, but beyond this she barely exists in history. She dedicated her book to her friends of the botanical bent, as a visual aid for their studies. And cyanotypes, like Atkins herself, are silhouettes, far less detailed than drawings, despite their perfectly replicated scale, despite their documentary nature. They leave a great deal to the imagination.

THE TOPOGRAPHY OF HIS CHIN

In 1867 Julia Margaret Cameron made a portrait of John Herschel. Like all her photographs, its tone is velvety sepia. Herschel's white hair sticks out of his cap like frost on straw. His eyes catch light, looking beyond the frame, beyond the visible world. Shadows gather in soft folds beneath his eyes. The sharpest focus is on his white-stubbled chin.

Of her photography habit, Cameron said, "I longed to arrest all the beauty that came before me and at length the longing has been satisfied."

The statement seems strikingly out of date: nowadays it is rare to consider one's longings satisfied. A feast only stretches the stomach. A word, however perfectly chosen, only shivers and slips away, splinters into a network of associations. *Scratch my back*, I ask my love. I bend my own arm behind me to point at the spot, and he scratches, compliantly. But always it's *A little to the left. A little higher.*

ON THE ACTION OF THE RAYS

Once upon a time, during a partial solar eclipse, Aristotle looked at the ground and saw the eclipse projected upon it. The moon was passing between earth and sun, making a crescent-shaped fireball that no one could look at directly. The sun shined through an aperture of leaves and drew itself with the moon as an upside down crescent, and Aristotle was puzzled by this phenomenon, the first recorded instance of a camera obscura.

Why is it that an eclipse of the sun, if one looks at it through a sieve or through leaves, such as a plane-tree or other broadleaved tree, or if one joins the fingers of one hand over the fingers of the other, the rays are crescent-shaped where they reach the earth?

Light moves like a well-shot arrow.

My friend built a camera obscura in an abandoned house at the edge of town. I knew the house as she described it, on the north side as you drove into town from the interstate. Most of the windows were broken, and shredded curtains blew in and out. I was never in that particular house, but like my friend, it was my habit or my hobby to drive out onto the plains where my voice carried far without anyone hearing it, where there were occasionally small abandoned houses with collapsed tar paper roofs, and I would go inside to try to capture something of their silence and light with my camera.

The floors of these houses were scattered with guano and bird shit and broken glass and rabbit pellets and small green plants that twisted up between floorboards. Maybe there was a frying pan in the sink, but the water didn't run. A leather boot in the toilet. Every time I entered one of these houses, I held my breath for a while, and then forgot and breathed normally. I kicked nails and gravel across the floor. I studied the decaying scraps of a quilt.

In a small room of my friend's camera house, she taped black paper over the window—it was remarkably intact—leaving a pinhole through which the light entered. The sun came through the branches of a dry cottonwood outside and cast an upside-down image on the wall, a network of tangles that moved with the wind. She taped white paper to the back wall to trace the tree, to make a perfect drawing like she had heard Vermeer may have done. But the branches moved, and the focus was soft and the drawing came out strange, as if she had drawn a spiderweb with her eyes closed. As if she had drawn enlarged varicose veins. Even tipped upright it did not look like tree branches against the sky. Her eye was inaccurate, unable to fill the gaps, unable to see what was really there.

But when I imagine the breathless hush of that house with the tree in it, upside down and joined with the peeling wallpaper and the rusted pipes, I don't care about the strangeness or softness of her drawing. I see the tree as she must have seen it. I imagine the decayed quilt, the frying pan, the shadows of a life once lived.

A FUGITIVE COLOR WILL DISAPPEAR

In an alchemist's lab in Berlin, 1704, a painter named Diesbach mixed saltpeter and cream of tartar, but the saltpeter was impure, oily with oxblood or animal bits. The paint—meant to be crimson— came out purple, an accident of tainted salts, gathered from who-knows-where. Maybe an ox stumbled at the mines and tore its hoof and the salt was scraped and gathered and sold anyway.

The intended red paint was called "lake," called "fugitive." It would have been impermanent, quick to fade in sunlight. Red lake was made with the acids of the cochineal insect, a South American bug that feeds on cacti. The male cochineal has wings, but the female simply digs her mouthparts into the cactus. She goes nowhere, but her body was crushed to make paintings of Jesus, for the scarlet robes of angels and saints. And such is our lust for color. Cochineal is in our food dyes—frosting, cheddar cheese, jam—and with it women paint their lips. They lick the stray smudges from their teeth.

Instead of red lake, Diesbach made Prussian blue.

IN THE YOUNG STATE, IN FRUIT

A cyanotype looks like a movie of your memory projected on the wall on a winter afternoon, late, low sunlight washing the corners. Anna Atkins had a collection of British algae, and one by one she pressed them beneath glass, against paper coated with Ammonium Iron (III) Citrate and Potassium Ferricyanide. She set the glass and paper in the sun, and the sun shone through the glass and through the leaves of the algae, through its tentacles and roots, through the clusters of its blossoms. Atkins rinsed the pages in water, and each sheet of paper bore the marks of sun and water around the shape of the algae, pale at the center of the deep blue page.

Atkins's cyanotypes are of ocean gardens, of underwater dreams, silent but for the bubbles of one's breath breaking the surface above. Later, Atkins made images of intricate ferns and petals of poppies, their stems tangled, their tightly closed buds like sperm with whipping tails.

THE ROMANTIC SENSIBILITY

If the roots of the plant are the human unconscious, and the flowers are our yearning for the divine, reaching and reaching and reaching, then what is the earth? We people become its appendages, little figures with dirty feet, and it becomes the collective unconscious, our source and place of union. But we reach, straining for something— for sky—even as we draw the earth's nutrients into our bodies.

THE WONDERS OF INDUSTRY

In 1851 a new building sprang from the London ground, all glass and steel and enclosed trees. Everyone gathered there: Anna Atkins and Charlotte Brontë and Charles Dickens and Matthew Brady and Charles Darwin and George Eliot—they all went to see the Great

Exhibition. The glass building was packed. Shoulder to shoulder they strolled beneath the glass, in a surprising hush, curious and thrilled. They marveled at caskets filled with pearls, at velvet-covered tables strewn with gold, at the inner-workings of trains. They leaned close to inspect daguerreotypes, surgical instruments, and microscopes. Everything was being made, being built, being cut, cast, polished, and assembled. And through the glass roof, there was the sky. They watched clouds drifting past. And time went on hurtling.

CALL US NOT WEEDS

Anna Atkins and Anne Dixon were girls together, almost sisters. This much Atkins wrote down. Later, when they were married women, they must have gathered their skirts and waded into tide pools side by side. Must have plunged their hands deep, picked sand from the tendrils of the plants they found, gently dug them out at the roots and laid them flat on tissue.

It was Anne Dixon who came when Anna's father died. He was nearly a father to her, too, having raised her alongside his own daughter, his Anna, so Anna's husband asked Anne to come. This, too, is written down. But how would it have gone?

"I don't know what to do with her," Anna's husband might have said. "She spends all day buried in her father's papers. She no longer takes walks. Her pillow is always damp. Please."

So Anne came.

It is not written, but my imagined Anna Atkins had a study, not a "drawing room." Not a parlor but her own room full of shelves and specimens and jars and pencils and bottles full of chemicals. And it is the door to this study that Anne Dixon would have flung open when she arrived to lift Anna from her grief.

"Darling girl," she might have said, her hands on her hips, though she and Anna were no longer girls. Anna's eyes were red and puffy and her hair thinning and tangled. She hadn't even pinned it up. Her face looked like a cabbage, folded. "Come with me now. You need some air."

The day was cool and hazy. The two women examined the crisp remains of summer's flowers. Anne picked a Yellow Rattle and shook it, the seeds scattering like rice after a wedding.

Movement was the thing they could not draw, could not press between glass and paper, could not capture with sunlight and chemicals. And Anne, as I imagine her, was fleet. Anne was a woman always turning away, always walking out into the field, always bending to look at a specimen instead of holding your gaze. She crouched to examine the veins of a leaf, the structure of a seedpod. She stood and whirled off like a dandelion seed.

But what is known of Anne Dixon? What is written? She was a cousin of Jane Austen, but they were not close. She helped Anna with her second book, the cyanotypes of ferns and flowers. The script that labels the images is thought to be hers. But Anne Dixon is a ghost, a trace walking at the edge of the frame.

This much is written: she died and was buried in a churchyard beside her husband. She had no children.

ORCHID MIMICS WASP, WASP MIMICS ORCHID

Plants depend on us. We are seduced by sugarcane, by tomatoes and apple trees. We are manipulated into thinking that we need them. But then, we do need them, their starches and their fibers and—most of all—their sugars. To eat only meat, only milk, only cheeses or creams—the thought makes me thirsty. Plants taunt us with their berries, their sweetness or bitterness, their bright flowers and clustered florets. They seduce us into harvesting them, into sowing their seeds. They lure bees to pluck their pollen, to carry them to the next plant, to the next blossom, to do the work they cannot do for themselves.

When my plants die—and this year so many of them have died: the snakeplants, the small pine tree that always dropped its needles, a tangled air plant, a jade that had grown from a cutting—I feel terribly guilty. I keep them around, shriveled and dry, for weeks. And when, in the vegetable bin, a red onion sprouts spring green shoots, I prop it up on a wooden cutting board. I photograph it each week, and the shoots grow to be over a foot tall, devouring the purple bulb. The house begins to smell of onion. It is a beautiful plant.

Recently my love and I decided to stop preventing pregnancy. If, someday, I have a child, I hope she does not inherit my brittle fingernails, my sun-sensitive skin, or my anxiety. I hope her hair is like that of my love, the man who scratches my back. We will not often comb it. And if I look through a telescope in 2065, I might focus on the planet where she lives, this daughter with tangled hair. I will focus on the planet where she cultivates edible mosses. Or maybe, instead, she will be the one that tilts the eyepiece toward me, both of us earthbound. And she will heat water for tea, then zip her jacket and go out for a walk through the night.

But maybe I will not have a child.

JUICES OF THE FLOWER OR LEAVES OF THE PLANT

When Anna opened the pages of her herbarium, she saw that the specimens had bled through the pages, staining the opposite page with their mirror image, although in some cases the color of the imprint differed starkly from the color of the plant. It is surprising the way the colors of plant juices change as they dry, but then, so does human blood, often darkening nearly to black as it hardens. And the dried color and texture depends largely on the surface to which it has been applied.

In the herbarium, the colors were mostly greens and yellows, some of which dried to brown or olive, or faded out almost entirely. The pages never dried flat but were bulky with the smashed, brittle plants pressed between them. But when Anna Atkins lost her child, the blood that traced the edge of the washbasin was deep red, only slightly more violet than it was when it left her body.

A child is like a plant, an algae flower in a salty sea. My Anna wanted one: a child. But she never again wanted to see the color of her blood change as it dried on her skin or on the edge of the basin or on the wooden planks of the floor from which it was impossible to wipe, the planks so porous and cracked that they wore the blood like varnish in the grain.

SPONTANEOUS GENERATION

Once upon a time, it was thought that tapeworms were born of the bodies of their hosts and that dead flesh generated maggots. Jan Baptist van Helmont (1580–1644) recorded a recipe for mice:

> 1 damp towel
> + wheat
> + time (21 days)
> + sunshine
> + scorpions
> + basil
> =1 batch of mice

Why do I imagine that Anna Atkins miscarried a child? Perhaps I assume that all British women in the nineteenth century wanted children, that all of them were defined by motherhood. Perhaps the plants are manipulating me again, swaying me with their fecundity and fertility, shaping, even, this imagined Anna. The language of reproduction is agricultural: all seeds and husbandry, cultivation and fruit. While nineteenth century British women were discouraged from pursuing scientific knowledge, botany was safe territory. Because a woman's body is the land from which the fruit sprouts? Because women are "of the earth"? It's not outrageous to imagine that Atkins wished for a child, but why do I imagine that she lost one this way? To miscarriage? There are many ways to lose a child, and it is likely she never contained one, never conceived.

But my imagination, rife with tragic narrative, walks the shore with the wind and the sunshine, and ruins another perfectly good essay. My imagination jumps into tide pools and pulls up orange and purple starfish. My imagination rolls down the dunes and coats itself in sugary sand.

Six months ago, in April, my own Anne Dixon—the friend that would wade with me in tide pools—birthed a stillborn baby girl, the baby's heart gone silent at eight months. And today I wait for this friend to call from her distant city, to tell me about her visit to the surgical obstetrician who will study the ultrasound, who will determine the quality of the polyp they have found within her, who will interpret the numbers that measure her hormones, the quality of her blood, the possibility for a child.

I wait. I walk alone. I turn the pages of a book of cyanotypes. I check on the oyster mushrooms I am growing in a pail in the kitchen.

STEAL MY HEART, RICHMOND, INDIANA

OVERGROWN STAIRWAY

(Between South Second Street and the Whitewater Gorge)

I make my way along the old railbed where the train used to run on the eastern edge the Whitewater Gorge. The train rolls through town on a different track now, but on quiet nights, or when the wind is blowing in the right direction, its whistle is still clear from my apartment. Before, the whistle would have been close enough to startle me awake. My windows would have rattled.

This is a crumbling postindustrial town, but it used to be bustling. They built cars and lawn mowers and pianos, wove cotton underwear. Roses bloomed in acres of glass greenhouses. Now I know this place by the scent of burning plastics one day, dog food on another.

I stand on the railbed looking over the gorge. In the first half of the twentieth century, workers would have used the old walkway that passes beneath me. They would have descended the stairway on their way to the piano factory or the recording studio. Nowadays, in summer, the railbed and stairway are overgrown with grass and weeds and leafy branches, and I don't walk here. But it is fall today, the first really cold weekend of the season, and the leaves have mostly fallen, clearing the view from the trestle to the river.

The upper opening of the walkway is mostly filled by dirt and vegetation, though there's still space enough for rainwater and animals to slip beneath it. I scoot down from the tracks on a concrete support structure. On the low side, the closed-up walkway is a sort of man-made cave scattered with garbage: soggy disposable diapers, empty cigarette packs, plastic bottles, candy wrappers. The walls are scribbled with graffiti. Green broken glass glints in the dirt. Someone might have camped out here for a time, or fucked, or smoked a bowl, or shot up. I make my way to the stairs, a tunnel through the leafless trees, down the slope to the gorge, too steep for safety, with no handrail. At the bottom of the steps, the gravel is split where rainwater has eroded a groove on its way to the river. Someone has dumped a pile of old shingles and siding.

They stopped pressing records here in the '40s, stopped making pianos in the 1950s. In the '70s, they tore down most of the six-story factory. Just last year the city tore up the rails on the trestle above me, leaving behind the overgrown pathway and a few creosote-coated ties.

The people who used this route are mostly dead now. These stairs are like a dying language. I have heard that one Plains tribe had a particular word for the ocular ridge around a bison's eye, but after the animals' numbers dwindled and the wide yellow fields stretched like a flat, unbroken sea, the word was forgotten. That could be apocryphal, but the point stands: if the thing a word names is gone, the word, too, disappears. I wonder if the converse holds true: can we forget a word to erase the thing it names?

I imagine the workers on their way to the piano factory. Men in coveralls or pants with suspenders. Women in wool skirts. They pause in their conversations as a train drowns out their voices. They swing lunchboxes as they stroll beneath the rattling boxcars. One whistles on his way down the steps. Of course, some of the walkers don't work in the factory at all but wait instead on the loading docks with shoeshine boxes or stacks of sandwiches, or they pass by the piano company on their way upriver to catch a few fish. Some are kids cutting across the gorge to school. Some are on their way to the studio to assist a trumpeter and singer named Louis Armstrong, who isn't quite famous yet, or Jelly Roll Morton, or Duke Ellington, all of whom will record some of their earliest songs here, pausing when passing trains shake the needle that scratches the music into wax.

But anyone can hire the studio. They also record KKK singers performing songs from their rallies. Some of these strolling, whistling workers who kneel to tie a shoe or bend to pick a stone out of their sock—these ghosts that tip their hats to me—are walking home to eat the dinner their wife has made, and then will go out again under cover of darkness, to a Klan meeting, or a rally, or worse. They breathe the scent of the burning torches. They feel the boil of hatred when they raise their voice in chorus.

To you ghosts moving past me on these stairs: I will the ice to grow slick under your boots. The rails on which your trains rolled, we have torn them out. These old ties are rotten, the trestle in ruins. Water erodes your walkway. Moss consumes the stairs. The trees reclaim them. I write these words so I don't forget that you walked here too, but I will not cut this pathway open again.

At the bottom of the stairs, a snap of branches. A rustling of leaves. I wonder if my ears know the difference between the sound of a startled deer and the sound of a person rolling over in a tent. I pause to listen but hear only chittering birds, water running underground, traffic humming on National Road—all distant. I stand at the center point of a radius of silence.

MARCELINE WANTED A BIGGER ADVENTURE

I would not have come across the grave of Marceline Baldwin Jones by chance. I like walking in the older, hillier section of Earlham Cemetery, where the crumbling graves are sometimes topped with the rain-softened shape of a lamb or praying hands, and the old Quaker names are in cursive scripts or simple block letters: Eliza and Caleb and Levi and Alice. Marceline's grave is in a newer section, an orderly corner far from the road, where the stones are organized like little villages, so their backs face each other and the heads of the dead rest together, sometimes arranged around the base of a tree. I looked up Marceline's grave on findagrave.com, and then located it on the cemetery map. I have visited deliberately, driven by twin habits of walking and curiosity. I do not know exactly what I am looking for.

It is a hot day in early spring, and I have sweated through my shirt. I have not brought water. I stand before the headstone. I see no evidence that anyone else has been here recently—no flowers or plants, no folded scraps of paper or envelopes. I hear the banging of a construction site somewhere far beyond the row of slender trees that marks the back edge of the cemetery. A few birds chirp.

Marceline Mae Baldwin was born in Richmond, Indiana, in 1927. She was a Methodist, a daughter and sister. She was, by all accounts, a generous and mild woman all her life. According to her cousin Avelyn Chilcoate, Marceline longed for a life outside the

159

small town; the two young women, both nurses, had plans to move elsewhere together, maybe to somewhere in Kentucky. But then, in 1948, Marceline met a strange young man named Jim Jones, an orderly at the hospital where she worked, and together they stepped into the stream of history.

Jimmy Jones was born in 1931 and spent his earliest years living with his parents in a shack without plumbing in rural Indiana, not far from where Marceline is buried. They say he was a strange kid, and that he had a hard time making friends. They say he was very intelligent and obsessed with death and religion, that he occasionally performed funeral ceremonies for squirrels and rabbits, and that even as a teenager, he busied himself reading Stalin, Marx, Mao, Gandhi, and Hitler. Jimmy's father was a veteran of the First World War, his lungs severely damaged by mustard gas. He couldn't work because of his ragged breathing—there were times he could barely walk—but Jimmy's mother was ambitious and worked hard at whatever jobs she could get. For some reason, she did not allow her son in their house when she was out, so after school he wandered the streets, ducking into a store to steal a candy bar (which his mother would pay for on the weekend) or into the pool hall, where he might find his father, or he practiced dramatic sermons standing on a stump at the edge of the woods. Later, Jimmy coached younger boys at baseball, naming the local team after the Cincinnati Reds. When Jimmy was in high school, his mother left his father, and Jimmy moved with her to Richmond, Indiana, the small city on the border of Ohio where I have lived for the past three years. A serious young man, he sometimes preached on the streets in Richmond, a Bible tucked under his arm, and he graduated early from the public high school, which is still the city's only public high school and stands just across the river from my house. At sixteen, Jimmy got a job working nights at Reid Hospital, and it was there that he met the pretty, intelligent nurse with green eyes.

My first thought was that she was angelic, just glowing, shining, a will-of-the-wisp and obviously special. I wondered, "Whatever does she see in him?"

—Jeanne Jones Luther, cousin of Jim Jones,
on the first time she met Marceline

No smile, but a warm, worldly gaze that could hold you forever. She is truly stunning, so sure and deep. She is exactly what her young Jimmy Jones needs to become a man.

—Stephan Jones, son of Marceline and Jim Jones,
describing his parents as he sees them in a photo
taken during their courtship in the late 1940s

When Marceline was twenty-two and Jim was nineteen, they married and moved across the state. In the years that followed, Jim was in and out of college, in Bloomington and Indianapolis, at IU and Butler. Marceline continued working as a nurse, and for a time, Jim worked for a monkey-importing business, selling pet monkeys door to door in Indianapolis.

Early in their marriage, Jim admitted to Marceline that he didn't believe in her God, but when the Methodist church committed to a new platform focused on racial integration and the alleviation of poverty, among other values that agreed with Jim's socialism, Jim decided to become a student pastor at a Methodist church. Marceline was thrilled, somehow seeming to forget that he wasn't actually Methodist, and maybe wasn't even Christian. Jim was a gifted preacher, but soon he became dissatisfied with the structures and routines of Methodism. He began preaching on the revival circuit, where he developed the kind of drama and charisma that drew crowds and donations. He began to perform healings, pulling "tumors" from people's mouths like coins from sleeves, like rabbits from hats. (In reality, they were rotten chicken livers he had learned how to palm.) Finally, he opened a small Indianapolis storefront church of his own. His parishioners were mostly African American women, and his services included helping them solve everyday problems, such as writing letters to the electric company to restore their power. His congregation outgrew the storefront, and in time, he bought a downtown building recently vacated by a Jewish congregation. He named his church Peoples Temple, the apostrophe deliberately omitted because apostrophes indicate possession—ownership. The people of the temple were black and white, young and old, and Jim Jones was their leader, their reverend, and a socialist.

"Jim has used religion to try to get some people out of the opiate of religion," Marceline explained in a 1977 interview, many years after she had come to terms with his lack of—and use of—Christian faith. Religion was a means to an end for him, a way to connect with the dispossessed. As for Marceline, she remained a faithful Methodist for a long time, but it isn't clear to me whether she still believed in a Christian God when she died.

Marceline gave birth to one son, whom they named Stephan, in 1959. Over the years, she and Jim adopted six other children: an eleven-year-old girl who may have been part Native American, three Korean orphans, a white American boy, and in 1961, a black American boy they named Jim Jr. They were the first white couple in Indiana to legally adopt a black child, and they called their family a "rainbow family." Jim and Marceline were deeply committed to civil rights and egalitarianism, and Jim was appointed to the Human Rights Commission of Indianapolis. But all this, of course, was only the beginning of their story, and these things are mostly forgotten now.

In a deeply segregated city, [Peoples Temple] was one of the few places where black and white working-class congregants sat together in church on a Sunday morning. Its members provided various kinds of assistance to the poor—food, clothing, housing, legal advice—and the church and its pastor, Jim Jones, gained a reputation for fostering racial integration.
—Rebecca Moore, professor of religion and sister of Carolyn Layton and Annie Moore, devoted members of Peoples Temple who both died at Jonestown

His message was always very stark . . . brotherhood, all races together. You were accepted just as you were, you were not judged by the way you looked, or how much education you had, or how much money you had.
—Rick Cordell, early member of Peoples Temple

Jim Jones combed his black hair in a soft wave that dipped over his left eyebrow. His part was straight, and he kept his sideburns neatly trimmed. His nose was round and his cheeks were fleshy. He was a good-looking man—face full enough, eyes warm enough. He wore a sport coat and sunglasses, always the sunglasses.

Marceline shares a headstone with her parents. Walter and Charlotte Baldwin had visited their daughter in Jonestown in 1978, only weeks before she drank the poison, and then she was gone. I imagine them purchasing the plots and the stone, their own deaths still years in the future though their daughter's life was over at the age of fifty-one. Two of the Jones children—Lew Eric and Agnes Pauline—are buried beside their mother. Their stones are set slightly apart from hers, almost as if to protect their privacy in death. They were adults themselves—aged twenty-one and thirty-five—when they died in Jonestown, and they had children of their own who also died that night. Lew's son, Chaeoke Warren Jones, was a year and a half old when he died, which means he would be my age now if he had lived. He is buried in a memorial site in Oakland, California, along with his mother, Terry Carter Jones, and many of the unclaimed or un-identified victims of the massacre.

As for Jim Jones himself, no one wanted his body buried in their cemetery, their town, their state. At first, the Baldwins and Jim's two surviving children planned to bury him in Earlham Cemetery with his wife and two children, but the people of Richmond protested. His body was sure to draw an unsavory element, as well as possible vio-lence at the funeral. Along with the rest of the bodies from Jonestown, his body was first flown from Guyana to Dover Air Force Base, in Delaware, but the people on the East Coast didn't want him buried in their states either. Some states devised sudden laws about whose bod-ies could and couldn't be interred within their bounds to ensure he would not be buried in their soil. In the end, his body was cremated, and his two surviving children scattered the ashes over the Atlantic.

In part, Marceline's grave is just a destination for a walk in a town where I have walked the same routes too many times, a town where I am sometimes bored by the walks, sometimes saddened by them— the boarded windows and potholes, the dogs that snarl and fling themselves at fences as I pass. I suppose I am walking here to med-itate on Marceline, though I do not valorize her. She is mostly a mystery to me. Thinking about her makes me wonder about loyalty and love and how they can blind us, about agency and belief, about devotion and delusion. Perhaps I am only a lookie-loo, seeking her grave to stand safely near tragedy without truly experiencing it, to feel the buzz of some electrical darkness. It has been forty years since the deaths at Jonestown. There is nothing here but names on stones, bodies deep in the earth, invisible, still, and decayed.

When I was twelve, my dad took a new job, and my family moved from a small town in Wisconsin to a Denver suburb, where the yards were fenced and treeless, the grass brown much of the year. The cost of living was higher than it had been in Wisconsin, and my sisters and I were old enough that it made sense for my mom to go back to work full-time. Our new home was, according to me and my sisters—and maybe my parents too, though they kept quiet about it—an ugly "suburban hell," and my sisters and I spent our unsupervised after-school hours indulging in MTV and other television we'd never been allowed to watch before. I still know well the songs and music videos that were popular in 1989, that first year in Colorado. Metallica's "One" tells the story of a World War I soldier who loses his limbs, sight, hearing, speech, and soul to a land mine. I was haunted by the image of a quadriplegic body draped in a sheet and isolated in darkness on its hospital bed. Skid Row's "Eighteen and Life" captured my imagination like a cheap novel, depicting a young life far more desperate and violent than my own middle-class existence. In these narratives, I recognized suffering, and I recognized my own safety and privilege.

Shortly after the move, my parents joined Amway, a pyramid scheme in which all members "own their own business" and earn a percentage of every product ordered by the business owners who join after them—beneath them on the pyramid. For a couple of years, my folks spent hours listening to cassette tapes that offered tips on how to approach friends, family, and strangers to get them to attend their meetings and join the business. At least one night a week they hosted a meeting in our living room, or attended one in the living room of their "sponsor," the person they'd joined under, or in the living room of one of the business owners near to them in the pyramid. The goal was always to bring a few "prospectives" to the meeting and get them to join. I spent many evenings babysitting a one-year-old named Kelsey—a baby whose habits and expressions I grew to know well, a baby I grew to love—while her parents attended meetings with my parents. My dad shaved his beard during those years, because Amway told him a clean-shaven face was a more successful and appealing business face.

One summer, my parents rented an RV and our family traveled to Spokane, where my parents attended the Amway Family Reunion, a convention where people like my parents listened to speakers meant to inspire them to get rich, and to teach them just how to do it. While my parents attended meetings, I babysat Kelsey in the hotel. On the final morning, a Sunday, we attended a church service in the hall where the meetings had taken place. Amway had their own worship band, the Goads—even the band name was a spur, reminding you to get off your ass and sell and praise and live your best capitalist life. I think it was after the church service that we accepted an open invitation to visit the home of one of the top businessmen in the organization, who lived nearby. I had my picture taken in his garage beside his red Corvette.

Amway seemed a cocktail of capitalism, self-help, and religion. *Make money for your family. Be your best American self. Get rich while helping others get there too!* I don't hear much about Amway these days, but in the years after my parents let their branch of the business dwindle and die, I heard it mentioned now and then, usually as the punch line to a joke about rubes or sleazy businessmen.

I often wonder how my parents escaped the jokes and derision of Amway, why they were naive enough to join. They joined in the organization's heyday, but still: wasn't it the sort of thing you stayed away from with a knee-jerk "no thank you," the same way you might hang up on a telemarketer? I think my parents did make a little extra money in those years, getting a percentage back on the products they bought that they would have bought anyway—the list of products was endless, everything from laundry detergent to cereal bars to plaque-fighting chewing gum—but how had they fallen for it? How had they so fully given themselves over, believing that they too could be millionaires, or at least a little wealthier, believing they'd earn college tuition for my sisters and me, or the sports car neither of them had ever desired?

When they quit, they argued about it. My mom wanted to keep their spot in the pyramid, making their small profit off products, but my dad wanted a clean break. Those in a pyramid scheme make no real friends; each person is using the others for financial benefit, and after they quit, my parents spent a lot of time making formal apologies, calling friends and family they'd propositioned and then lost touch with, presumably because they'd offended them. My dad apologized to me and my sisters, too, for spending so much time on it, for letting those years pass too swiftly, with too much focus in the wrong places. It seemed there was something sticky in my parents' argument about quitting—some paradigm had lured them and shifted their vision, an illusion they now had to dismantle and release. Amway isn't a cult, and no one was going to ask them to drink poison, but it was a scheme that demanded they entangle their hopes for the future, their family, and even their faith, with their finances. It asked too much to be a safe venture.

For some months in the early 1960s, the Joneses lived in Brazil, one of the places Jim believed would survive nuclear holocaust, based on an article he had read on the topic in *Esquire* magazine. And then there was the big move of Peoples Temple from Indiana to Ukiah, California, another area listed in the *Esquire* article. The people called Jim "Father," and Marceline was "Mother." Jim told Marceline—and his followers—that maybe he was God. Jim told his people to sign over their money and their goods, their social security checks. Sometimes, if they disobeyed, he beat them. There were drugs—lots of drugs—and Jim had sex with the men and the women of his temple. Some people left. Some people filed complaints. But the temple also helped people recover from addictions, and fed them, and helped them get jobs, and paid for them to go to college. It was an interracial, socialist family that shared what it had with every member, no matter their race or background.

Although Marceline couldn't bear any more children, she loved the ones she had, both adopted and biological. Her back ached with rheumatoid arthritis, and she couldn't have sex anymore, or not very often, but she stayed married to Jim even after he openly took a lover. Jim lived with Marceline for part of each week.

When I think about Marceline, I think about the strange avenues of our lives, the unexpected digressions, the ways, in retrospect, our paths can seem both fated and surprising, an impossible balance of magic and choice.

Never did I imagine I would live in Richmond, Indiana, a town to which I moved because there is a college here, where I am a visiting assistant professor. I am forty-one years old, childless or—depending on how I spin it, depending on the day—child-free. I am standing in a cemetery at the grave of Marceline Baldwin Jones, a woman to whom I have no specific connection, but I would like to leave something here—flowers, a scrap of silk, a marble—some token that says *Rest in peace my puzzle,* or *Someone was here. I remember you.*

Who else has stood here and marveled that they are standing at the grave of a woman they never knew, at the surprises of Marceline's life, the surprises of their own? And who has stood here who knew Marceline and wondered all the more at her unlikely path?

Stepping closer to Marceline's headstone, I now notice two pennies, heads up, resting on the back ledge, evidence that others wanted to leave something too. But my pockets are empty. No dandelions or violets grow here. I have only a small notebook, a pen, and my phone.

In 1977 an article in *New West* magazine made public some of the darker secrets of Peoples Temple. Former members reported that they had been harassed and coerced, that public humiliation and physical abuse of temple members were par for the course, that under threat of abuse and humiliation members were forced to donate belongings and property, including the deeds to their homes, that Jones faked healings of temple members, and that once he had feigned being shot so that he could also feign healing his own gunshot wounds. The temple ran a number of youth homes that received funding from the state, and a couple who had supervised one of the homes reported that state money meant for the care of boys who lived in the home was given instead to the temple.

Jones got wind of the article before its publication and, bracing for the fallout, he and hundreds of his followers moved to a settlement in Guyana, a newly independent Socialist country where the people were mostly black and English was the official language. The relocation had been in the works since 1974, when the temple had leased more than three thousand acres of Guyanese land on which to build their communist utopia. A smaller group of Jones's people had been in Guyana for over a year, working to establish the settlement. The *New West* article raised doubts that everyone in Guyana was there of their own free will and questioned whether people would be able to leave should they decide Jonestown was not the life they wanted.

Deep in the jungle, the settlers built small frame houses and tried to grow food, and they named their village Jonestown after their leader. Jim Jones ruled over it, and ruled over them. He spoke to them for hours over a loudspeaker, late into the night after they had worked hard all day. He lived with Carolyn Layton and Maria Katsaris, his two long-term lovers. For a time, Marceline stayed in California, leading Peoples Temple there and defending her husband to the press and the government. In October of that year, she moved to Jonestown, though she often flew to Washington, DC, to defend her husband before Congress or the courts. Sometimes, when Jones was feeling especially ill or drugged or had another commitment elsewhere, Marceline—Mother—spoke for him.

When I was twenty, in college, my parents came to visit me on a Sunday, and I took them to church with me. They had raised me Catholic, but I had been attending a nondenominational Christian church that gathered in the high school a few blocks from my house. We walked in the front doors of the school, past the taxidermied impala, a type of antelope that lives in southern Africa with long, thin legs and lyre-shaped antlers, for some unfathomable reason the school mascot.

We entered the auditorium. Spotlights lit the stage, where the worship band played songs with a lot of major chords. People waved their hands and closed their eyes and sang. I, too, closed my eyes and sang, and sometimes I raised my hands and imagined God's love as warm and yellow, like sunlight through my heart. The pastor, Johnny Square, was a compact, athletic man, always stylishly dressed in a suit, a passionate speaker. Johnny Square called on us to take some particular action that demonstrated our faith. He challenged us— and said that to disobey him would be to disobey God.

A few weeks later, my dad sent me a letter, though he lived only an hour away and I saw him regularly, and we sometimes also spoke on the phone. He wrote that he was worried for me, that he worried about my passion and idealism, that he knew how easy it was to follow powerful emotions, that he worried about obedience when it was demanded by a preacher, that he worried about cults.

I suppose a part of me was angry about the letter—at the lack of trust it exhibited, or at the challenge to my independence, as well as to my faith in Johnny Square, a man I had respected and considered a spiritual leader. But I don't remember the anger. I remember I thought my dad was sort of right.

For months before the letter arrived, my faith had been shaky. There were things about Christianity that I just didn't believe, and didn't like, and I had been trying out churches, riding my bike to a different one each week, seeking one that felt right, that really fit my idea of God and faith. My skirt would get tangled in the spokes as I rode, and I would arrive disheveled and feeling shy. I had started to skip a week now and then, and then I skipped more weeks than not. I shaved my head, something mildly symbolic of grief and newness. I took a lot of hikes and runs, and I spent countless hours behind my camera, photographing burnt trees and roadside firework stands and plastic baby dolls and orange peels. I spent entire nights, entire weekends, in the darkroom printing photographs. Gradually, in this way, art replaced my religious faith. I remember what it was like: not a sudden revelation, but a slow unwinding, a letting go.

Do I see in Marceline something of myself? Another path I could have taken, had I been born in a different time, had I found the perfect pastor, even—or especially—one whose faith was based on communism and not the Bible?

In the US, suspicion and worry about Jones and Peoples Temple gained steam. Family members of Jonestown residents formed a group, called the Concerned Relatives, and wrote letters to the Guyanese government and the US secretary of state, urging an investigation. In 1978, led by former temple lawyer Tim Stoen, the Concerned Relatives launched a human rights lawsuit against Jones, who quickly countersued for damages.

Complicating matters, Tim Stoen's five-year-old son, John, was in Jonestown and was at the center of a bitter custody battle. Jones claimed he was the child's father, and perhaps he was. Stoen had signed an affidavit stating that it was true, but perhaps he had done so under coercion—not an uncommon tactic for Jones. Stoen's wife, Grace, had left Peoples Temple in 1976, and her testimony against Jones was included in the *New West* article. Tim Stoen had remained a member of the temple and moved to Guyana with John. But in 1978, Tim Stoen, too, defected (or escaped), and joined Grace's custody battle. Courts ruled in their favor, but Jones refused to release the boy, even though the court ruling meant that he would be arrested if he returned to the US without surrendering the boy.

In the fall of 1978, California congressman Leo Ryan, heeding the requests of the Concerned Relatives, contacted Jones and expressed his wish to visit Jonestown. The request made Jones angry and nervous. It was Marceline who pleaded with him to be reasonable. *We have nothing to hide*, she said. *Why shouldn't he visit? We will show him what we're doing, and that people are not kept here against their will.* Eventually, Leo Ryan visited. The visit went horribly awry; on November 18, 1978, one of the people of Jonestown shot the congressman dead on a runway in the jungle of Guyana.

Marceline Baldwin was born in Richmond, Indiana, and her body was returned to this place where I stand, a place that no one much knows or recognizes. Google immediately defaults to Virginia when you type "Richmond." But everything begins somewhere, and Jonestown began here, when Jim Jones met Marceline Baldwin, a woman with intelligence, compassion, social grace, and beauty. Her father was on the city council; she knew how to move among the educated classes and the politicians, and Jim learned from her. A typical midwesterner, she was loyal to a fault. I think of Tammy Wynette's 1968 hit song, "Stand by Your Man," how Jim's good times paralleled Marceline's bad ones—until the times were bad for everyone. Afraid or miserable, betrayed or heartbroken, she had children with him, and she believed in his mission of equality and socialism. She stayed.

Is this part of what it means to be curious? I want to know about the pale bark of sycamores, a tree I don't remember seeing in the West, and about the ways people in different geographic regions slice their pizza (in Indiana: squares), and about the unknowable and surprising pathways of our lives. I live in here, in Richmond, Indiana, where Jim Jones once preached on street corners and Marceline Baldwin nursed people back to health. And so I read about Peoples Temple and about Jonestown. I look up the location of Marceline's grave and I walk to it. This is another way of knowing a place: I follow my curiosity with my feet. Marceline's stone and the strange path of her life are the shapes over which I drape my curiosity today.

I met the man who is now my husband at the wedding of our two best friends. After the wedding, we were at a pub with the bride and groom and other wedding guests, and in the din, he told me about his childhood in a commune, a "community" in which his parents still lived. He was delivered by a midwife in a cabin his dad had built on the shared community land in California, not far from the ocean. He was the first child born within the community, and when they knew he was a boy, his dad went out and waved a blue flag from the top of a hill to let the others know. My husband spent his first years in California among tepees and hand-built shacks and gardens. Potty training meant learning to use the outhouse, which scared him because it was full of spiders. He spent his days running naked with the other community children.

This was in the mid-1970s. In the early '80s—only a few years after the deaths at Jonestown—the community sold the California land, where they were stretched by bad financial decisions and harassed by fearful neighbors. They moved to rural Nevada, and after a year, most of them moved to Salt Lake City, where the community remained for the rest of my husband's childhood, supporting itself with a chain of natural food stores and other small businesses.

Sometime between California and Salt Lake City, my husband's mother became sick, and in prayer she promised that if she was healed of her illness, she would remain faithful to their spiritual leader, Norm, and to the community, where everyone meditated twice a day and believed in prophets and energy and love. She was eventually diagnosed with Graves' disease. Her thyroid was irradiated, and she has regulated her hormones with levothyroxine ever since. She remained committed to the community and her faith, even after Norm died, and even after her husband wanted to leave the community.

As my husband grew up, the community changed financial models many times, shifting from shared finances to more independent finances, and with each new iteration, people left the group. When I met my husband, the community had moved back to California and owned a handful of stores there and in Arizona. There weren't many people still living on the land with the group, but many people visited them regularly for meditation or joined them for retreats. His parents stayed through it all, meditating twice a day, working for the stores or the church or the land.

When he told me part of this at the pub after our friends' wedding, I was intrigued. I'm a sucker for a good story, and as he spoke I imagined him as a suntanned baby in California, running among goats and flowers and guitars. But little of what I learned about the community in the months and years that followed, or when we visited his parents, aligned with my previous ideas about communes. The community members are teetotalers, for one, and Norm all but forbade extramarital or premarital sex. Their religion is an amalgamation of Eastern and Western beliefs and practices. Over the years, there were many betrayals, both financial and personal. There were broken friendships and broken hearts. A couple of years after my husband and I married, his parents finally left the community. They still meditate every day, and they remain in touch with some of their old friends, but they live in Washington now, far from the people they worked, prayed, and lived with for more than forty years.

I note the similarities between my husband's family's community and Peoples Temple: The way that socialism shaped the members' lives and practices. The way they followed the directives of a single flawed and demanding man. The way some people stayed, no matter the losses and betrayals and poor business decisions. The way their faith demanded everything from them. And I wonder at the differences. My husband's parents' faith demanded their lives, but not their deaths. How does one see this invisible line? Would they have refused? Would I?

After the congressman was murdered on the runway, the community of more than nine hundred people gathered at the center of Jonestown. There was a large pot filled with dark liquid resting on a table—grape Flavor Aid mixed with cyanide. Jim Jones told his people to drink the liquid from little cups, but first to use preloaded syringes to press the liquid into the mouths of their children so that their children would not be tortured by the capitalists and the government. He told them it was not suicide but a revolutionary act that would communicate their socialist ideals to the world. They could not go on living in such an unjust society. And they put the syringes to their children's mouths, and they drank from the cups, and they lay down in the dirt, and they died.

Marceline found solace in her children.

—Jeff Guinn, *The Road to Jonestown*

All this, of course, is what we remember. Not socialism but "Kool-Aid." Not communism or public services or racial equality but fallen bodies, sneakers and dungarees and corduroys and T-shirts, so many bodies lined up and piled in the dirt. In photos taken from above, they appear like bags of garbage strewn across the land. The people of Jonestown dead together, facedown in the dirt.

On the recorded audiotapes from that night in Jonestown (they always recorded Jim Jones's speeches), Jim speaks to Marceline, saying, "Mother, Mother, Mother, Mother," asking her to stop crying and pleading. He asks her to obey, to drink the liquid, to die with the children, to die for the Cause. His voice is remarkably calm. After the children and the babies were dead—around three hundred of them—Marceline drank the liquid and died.

When I read about the tapes, I was surprised. I had always thought—though it was mystifying—that Marceline drank quickly and willingly, that everyone in Jonestown drank willingly, blindly, with devotion. I thought that to "drink the Kool-Aid" was to be a sheep, a gullible follower. But not everyone drank willingly. The group was surrounded by men with guns, and some of their bodies bore welts where they had been injected with cyanide when they refused to drink from the cups on their own. And the children died first, many of them at the hands of their own parents—an act more powerful than communism or socialism or God or Jim Jones. The children died first at the hands of the adults. How, after that, could the parents go on living?

Jim Jones died of a gunshot wound that he probably inflicted on himself. He did not press the syringe to his lips. He did not drink the juice from a little cup.

I think my mom did the best that she could do with what she had because it was all that she could do . . . there were a lot of things that kept her there.
—Stephan Jones

Love of her children was foremost, as well as a sense of responsibility to all of Jones's followers, who she believed were good people, genuinely trying to change the world for the better.
—Jeff Guinn, *The Road to Jonestown*

Marceline Baldwin Jones was once in love with a man, her husband. She was idealistic, committed to fighting racism and sharing resources and caring for children. She was loyal. But her life, her death, her loyalty, became a chilling warning against holding too tightly to ideals. *Be moderate; love reasonably,* her story whispers, opposing every message of love and idealism and generosity I have ever heard. This whisper is part of what draws me to her story and to her grave, part of what puzzles me. *Why did you do it, Marceline? What happened to you, Marceline? Why this blind spot? Why did you stay?*

Reid Hospital in Richmond, Indiana, where Marceline Baldwin met Jim Jones, was built in 1905 and served this small city for more than a hundred years. In 2008 the hospital sold the buildings on the original site to a group of developers and moved into a new facility up the road. Through a series of bad decisions, worse circumstances, and greedy betrayals, the old hospital was twice handed off from the original development group to other developers, but eventually all plans fell through; the last pair of investors stopped paying taxes and all but vanished from Indiana. The abandoned buildings have been rotting ever since. By the time I moved to Richmond in 2015, the old hospital was a hulking ruin, shameful, overgrown and broken, jagged and spray-painted. Thieves had stripped it of its valuable metals and set fire to the structure more than once. Even in a town with plenty of abandoned buildings, the hospital was a riveting eyesore of toxic decay, a testament to poor management and Rust Belt poverty.

But after a decade of vacancy, the building is finally, as I write this, being demolished. The place where Jim Jones met Marceline Baldwin—the woman who would become his wife, who would model for him effective political behavior, who would make possible his ascendancy as leader of Peoples Temple, and who would die at his side in a jungle settlement in Guyana—within another month or two, that place will no longer stand. But I will not see the demolition to its completion. My move is already planned, and I will be gone from Richmond before the building is gone. There are poisons locked within the old structure—asbestos certainly, and maybe mercury and lead. It is a scar that will not heal before I leave.

But I stand in this cemetery, by Marceline's stone. I have read too much about her, about Jonestown and Peoples Temple. I have let whole days dwindle to darkness as I read, questions swirling, wondering why I cannot look away. But today, the woods behind Marceline's grave are beautiful and straight and still against the sky, and the first leaves of spring are bright, tender green in the understory, and now I walk toward them, into the forest.

PIETÀ: RICHMOND, INDIANA

My favorite pizza place in this town makes a crust that's not thick enough to be chewy, but isn't quite crisp either. I order it with green olives, which means salty enough to regret my choice when I wake up thirsty in the middle of the night. It's takeout only, no dining room.

If I pick up a pizza from Mercurio's and the guy with the eye patch isn't working the register, I'm seriously disappointed. I imagine him as the owner. The place is always full of smoke from the ovens, and a dozen or so workers are back in the open kitchen, sprinkling cheese and sliding pizzas into boxes. If you forget to ask them to slice your pizza into wedges, they cut it into squares. I've come to think of this as the midwestern way.

It happened on a Saturday night. A guy in a ski mask burst into the shop, but the owner was quick and shot him lickety-split. The robber crumpled on the front steps. The owner sat next to him and pulled him onto his lap, and the man died there, lying across Mercurio's lap like Jesus in the Pietà.

Mercurio is the name of the Roman messenger god, after which the thick, silvery liquid in an old-fashioned glass thermometer and the smallest planet in the solar system are named. Mercury has mostly been phased out of thermometer production now that it's understood to be toxic. I always misremember the name of Romeo's friend in *Romeo & Juliet* as Mercurio—the friend who first draws his sword at the Capulet ball but loses the fight. As he dies he shouts, *A plague on both your houses!*

There was no Pietà scene, of course, but that's how I prefer to remember the news story that I found by accident, while googling for the phone number the first time I called in an order. I don't want to know the ways I'm wrong, and I don't want to see the gun ads that will pop up in my browser's sidebar if I research the facts.

Of course, if Mercurio, my eye-patched owner, had handed over the cash that night, most likely no one would've died. The robber would have raced off in a getaway car, the workers catching their breath back in the shop, beginning to murmur to each other, the owner staring blankly at the empty register drawer. And yes, the robber would probably have held up another place the next week, and the next. There's no good way to spin this story.

But I don't want to look up the article so I can tell this story straight. This is the way I like to remember it: Mercurio looked down into the face of his enemy and smoothed the hair off his forehead, while the ambulance siren screamed in the distance—too slow, too slow.

BLIGHT (DISAMBIGUATION)

The exact number of blighted and abandoned properties in Indiana is unknown. Estimates have suggested there may be as many as 50,000.

—City of Richmond, Department
of Metropolitan Development

On the first cold weekend of fall, with months of cold and gray ahead, I set out on a walk—to damn the cold, to keep myself moving. I walk east, although I know that without the leaves and flowers of summer, the houses there cannot hide their crumbling faces and boarded windows, the trash that gathers in their fences, their heaps of dry brown leaves.

Since August 2015—the month I moved to town—the city of Richmond, Indiana, has torn down 138 dilapidated houses as part of the federally sponsored Blight Elimination Program. These were houses designated in "very poor" condition when scored on a matrix. A "very poor" house has structural damage—no roof, say, or serious fire damage.

I moved here on a one-year contract to teach creative writing at a small liberal arts college. Now in my third year of the job, but still a visiting assistant professor, I rent half of a duplex in Old Richmond.

I was surprised to learn that my neighborhood is one of those designated "hardest hit" by blight because many of the houses in my neighborhood are charming. Built mostly at the turn of the twentieth century, electric candles gleam in their windows and wrought iron fences line the walks. In fall, trees shower the streets and yards with bright leaves. The sidewalks are mostly herringboned brick, buckled by tree roots and overgrown with moss and weeds.

There are only a few abandoned homes in this twelve-block grid, and only a few empty lots, especially compared to the adjacent neighborhoods of Vaile and Starr, the direction in which I am walking. They are also designated "hardest hit," though just about every neighborhood in the central, older part of town bears the label. The newer homes are out on the curving streets and cul-de-sacs, away from the downtown storefronts that are largely vacant and stinking of mildew. The newer homes sit on subdivided plots—single-family homes with attached garages, more or less what you expect to find at the edges of any American city.

Blight is foremost a symptom affecting plants in response to infection. Bacterium, mildew, mold, fungus: the leaf, stem, or fruit browns or fades. The plant experiences chloriosis—it fails to produce chlorophyll. It was blight that destroyed the potatoes in Ireland in 1845. Specifically, it was *P. infestans*, amoeba that shrink potatoes from the outside and rot them from the inside. To treat blight, a farmer must act fast or they'll lose entire fields, entire crops. Infected storage bins can destroy the food supply for years.

For the past few years, the city of Richmond has paid $15,000 for a qualifying dilapidated house without a basement, $25,000 for one with a basement. Although there are many dilapidated homes remaining, the Blight Elimination Program is nearing its end—unless the city gets another grant. There have been three such grants, each one expanding the number of houses the city can afford to demolish.

Blight (disambiguation): These were houses infected with bacterium, mildew, mold, fungus, rainwater, fire, broken pipes, broken windows, boarded windows, crass graffiti, human feces smeared on doors and clapboard, paint peeling from bricks, trees sprouting through roof holes, drain pipes full of rotten leaves, gutters heavy with soil and moss, plastic tarps stretched over warped shingles—to keep out water, to slow decay, but now threadbare and billowing—porch railings that splinter and sag or are altogether missing, holes punched through floors and ceilings, stained clothes and newspapers pressed between windowpanes. These were faded and broken and empty houses standing beside other faded and broken and empty houses standing beside faded houses where people still live.

In most cases, the lots where houses were demolished are completely flat. Once in a while, though, where a house used to sit a few feet higher than the sidewalk on a raised lot, the little hill is still there, along with the steps that once led to its front door or walkway. Three or four concrete steps, no railings, sometimes flanked by mortared stone walls. Sometimes the steps are overgrown with grass and weeds. Sometimes they are swept bare. Usually, trash and leaves have collected in the corners. These stairs capture me: they are remnants of dwellings, like phantom limbs, aching with the memory of what once was. Once they held people up, they grasped their houses. The bodies are gone, but the limbs remain.

GHOST STAIRS: 335 S. 7TH STREET

Four risers and four steps, flanked by a pair of curved concrete walls, too new to be original to the lot. The stairs lead to a broken chain-link fence with no street-facing gate. Leaves pile in the corners of the lower two steps.

To the north: a brick garage painted bright red. To the south: *Iglesia La Luz del Mundo*, painted matte white. The name of the church is stenciled gold block letters in Spanish to the left of the door, in English to the right. Along the wall of La Luz, as if marking the boundary of the empty lot, is a line of children's play equipment: tricycles and big wheels, a crusty sandbox, the walls of a collapsed plastic play house. In summer, maybe the empty lot is the site of church picnics with lemonade and ice cream cones, corn roasted in the husks, and rented inflatable bounce houses, but now it's late afternoon on a Saturday in November. My hands are freezing as I focus my camera on the stairs to the empty lot.

I am firmly middle-aged, but I have never owned a home. On a year-to-year contract at the college, it has not made sense to buy a home here, although the houses are absurdly affordable. "Absurdly affordable" also means "difficult to sell" when you move, and so I rent. When the dishwasher breaks, I am glad I can call the property manager to request a repair, but someday I would like to have a garden in which I have improved the soil year after year, a living room in which the walls are painted a color I like, and if I punch nails into the walls to hang maps and photographs, they will not eventually cost me twenty-five dollars apiece. Sometimes I squint at the carpet in my apartment—bland, speckled brown, very forgiving of spills—and imagine how the place would look if the floors were shining wood. But the days pass quickly, with much to be done, and today, after this walk, I will apply for longer term jobs at colleges and universities in cities far from here.

When a house is approved for demolition, someone from the city spray-paints the word *OK* on it with red paint. This means that a house is not OK, will never be OK again. This red *OK* says *it is OK to destroy this one*, says it is better off gone. Although I have never seen the painter, it seems the tag is always sprayed by the same hand, the distinguishable font of a city employee, blocky capital letters with soft angles on the *K*, the letters always around eight inches tall. *OK* means *officially blighted*. And sadly, it is sometimes difficult to tell which houses are condemned—there are many dilapidated and abandoned houses, and not all of them are part of the program.

Sometimes occupied homes surrounded by dilapidated homes seem to overcompensate for their missing neighbors. The owners tuck colorful gourds into every curve of a wrought iron fence, string fairy lights from eaves, loop evergreen boughs over windows and doors, stuff a porch swing with pillows, fill their yard with a dozen grinning jack-o'-lanterns.

The OK'd houses are gnawed apart by excavators and flattened by bulldozers. The rubble is hauled away. The lots are plowed flat and planted with grass, the seed covered with a layer of yellow straw to keep it from blowing and protect it from hungry birds. The Vaile neighborhood, where I walk, and where many of the demolished houses once stood, is now dotted with empty lots, like a mouth with missing teeth.

These were homes where people ate dinner at the table, or in front of the blue flicker of the television. Where they slid across the floorboards in their socks. And yet, by the time the houses were torn down, they were—even for a person who loves old houses, who fantasizes about restoring one—unsalvageable. No one would buy them. No one could restore them. They were victims of a changed economy, of deindustrialization, corporatization, population decline, unemployment, poverty, subprime mortgages, and widespread drug addiction.

The line between a red *OK* and a house where a child eats breakfast on the sofa, a house where an old woman feeds the neighborhood cats at the same time every evening, is a line I can't always discern. It's thin and uneven. Perforated. Smeared.

The stated mission of the Blight Elimination Program is to save the houses that are still homes by removing the ones that are not. By pruning the infected limb, the city hopes to stop the plummeting of property values.

GHOST STAIRS: 132 S. 11TH STREET

Four narrow steps, completely overgrown. Either this was one of the first houses to go, or these steps have been missing their house since before the blight elimination program. Tall brown grasses gone to seed, bursting like fireworks.

Once, a chandelier gathered dust in the entryway. A fireplace flickered. A child learned to take all the steps in a single bound. Morning after morning, a rolled newspaper thumped. A friend shuffled up the walk with a casserole after a birth, after a death. As I focus the camera, four dogs bark and leap at the fence next door.

In the 1940s and '50s, the United States researched the possibility of using *P. infestans,* potato blight, as a biological weapon to destroy the enemy's food source, but in the end, the military hasn't used this weapon because it is too difficult to control the spread of blight. Eventually, we'd lose our potatoes too.

What would happen if, instead of spending thousands to tear down these houses, money was granted to homeowners—or neighbors—before the water heater breaks, before the roof collapses, before the foreclosure, the disgrace, the abandonment? It seems there must be another way. That there must be other ways.

GHOST STAIRS: CORNER LOT, S. B AND S. 13TH STREETS

A three-inch riser to a field of soft green grass, unmowed for weeks, maybe months. A single step, stunted and chipped, now an altar holding an overturned Styrofoam cup, a pair of crumpled cellophane wrappers, a napkin.

Once, (I imagine) a couple posed for a prom photo. He slipped the corsage onto her wrist and they angled their heads toward each other. She stood one step lower, his hand on her shoulder. Her dad squinted into the viewfinder, pressed the shutter. And another shot: he's on the lower step, looking up at her, holding her hand, a pink satin glove. The girl in the gloves imagines a future: gingham curtains, coffee percolator, three babies.

But it's only prom, and he is a terrible dancer. Pink Gloves wonders if that's enough reason not to accept an invitation for a second date. But he has other plans, anyway. A girl in Dayton with smooth black hair. Enough money for a shiny helmet and a motorcycle that he knows how to repair. In June, he straps his guitar to the bike and drives east.

I wander back and forth, walking the blocks of the Vaile neighborhood, noting the newly empty lots, dark dirt spread with a layer of yellow straw. I study the houses with rotting turrets, broken windows, dark porches. I wonder if I need a stronger prescription for my glasses. My head aches, and my own house seems endlessly far away.

GHOST STAIRS: 109 S. 13TH STREET

Mortared stone frames four steps where once someone slipped on the ice at the end of a long winter. Or maybe it was on the morning after the first frost, before she had gotten salt for the walk. It hadn't snowed—there was no need to shovel—but the stairs were slick and she was nearly seventy—*how had that happened?* She broke her goddamned hip, and once the hip goes, well, it's all downhill from there. But she limped for years before she couldn't walk at all, and there were years during which to grow familiar with the sight of her toes poking up beneath the blanket, watching the room regain its colors in the morning light.

Like the old woman I often see on E Street, not far from here, hunched so far over her walker I can't see her eyes. She can't look up. Her neck is too stiff, her spine too curved. A basket of laundry perches on the walker. She leans hard, the wheels dragging and scraping, her progress slow. But this isn't a place in which city buses trace endless lines through the streets, nor kneel to scoop up their passengers.

In most blight elimination programs, including the one in Richmond, cities must have a community partner or a plan for redevelopment before they tear down a house. In Michigan, cities are required to arrange partnerships with architectural salvage firms before they demolish houses, and to train and employ homeless people to work on demolition and beautification crews. In cities like St. Louis, where I once lived, and Cleveland, young people, neighbors, and restauranteurs plant gardens and harvest the food.

Still, many lots sit empty for years. But then, *empty* often means a span of lush green grass where a child throws a baseball to himself, a dog catches a Frisbee, young trees struggle toward the light. And yet I wonder if proactive policies might have saved some of these homes, might still save some.

I pass two different men lying on their backs in the street, tinkering beneath minivans, and children screaming on the slide in the school playground, motor scooters zipping past on a day too cold for motor scooters. I breathe the scents of burning leaves and rotting garbage. From the yards, aging jack-o-lanterns watch as I pass, their jagged grins collapsing on themselves like the toothless mouths of strange and ancient people.

A SPRING IS THE EYE OF THE LANDSCAPE

FIND A SPRING

It's Friday afternoon, the first really warm day in April, when I visit the artesian well in Glen Miller Park with my friend Jen, an anthropologist. Jen parks her car in the lot across from the artesian well and we bring our water bottles and notebooks across the stone bridge to the place where three silver pipes gush untreated water fresh from the earth. I bend to fill my bottle and note the tiny green plants that wave and float in the square concrete pool around the pipe, growing from pale, bulbous roots, like tiny chives. The water is cold and clear and perfectly flavorless.

The map on FindASpring.com inaccurately pins this spring at the southwest entrance of the park, near the Madonna of the Trail monument[1] in Richmond, Indiana, the town where Jen and I live with about thirty-six thousand other people, on the Ohio border, just east of Interstate 70. The aerial photo on the website was taken during summer, when the trees of our town were in full leaf and the grass

---

1 There are eleven other such monuments from Maryland to California, dedicated to the spirt of pioneer women and erected in the 1920s by the Daughters of the American Revolution. The monument is a concrete sculpture of a woman with children tangled in her arms and skirts. Her face is stern, eyes affixed to the uncertain distance ahead.

was much greener than it is now. In the photo, the streets appear as an orderly grid, vibrant and neat in a way that I have not experienced when walking or driving on them. Even when the world is green and blooming, there is garbage washed against the curbs and caught in chain-link fences, dirty vinyl siding, yards cluttered with forgotten things. At the corner of National Road[2] and North 22nd, across from the monument, stands the boarded-up Crane House with its half-shingled roof and blowing, faded tarps. So many lampposts are missing their lamps.

FindASpring.com shows the approximate location of reported springs and artesian wells all over the world, but many of the comments on the site reveal that various wells and springs have stopped flowing, or that people can no longer find them. Sometimes a commenter offers updated GPS coordinates, and then another commenter reports that they still can't find the well. But even with the inaccurate pin, the comments on our local watering hole are a mix of rave reviews, nostalgia, and warnings about possible chemical runoff and Total Dissolved Solids. The Glen Miller Park Spring is most definitely still flowing, well-used, and beloved.

BODIES OF WATER

The body of an adult human is approximately 60 percent water, with the average for men being higher than that of women. The average

---

2 Construction of the National Road—also known as US 40 today—began in 1811. It was the road that took settlers west from Cumberland, Maryland (near Washington, DC) to Vandalia, Illinois, sixty-three miles east of St. Louis, when the government ran out of money to finish the project. Today, I-70 allows travelers to speed past Richmond without so much as glimpsing the town, but the National Road is still the town's east–west artery, leading from the hotels, gas stations, and big-box stores on the eastern end, through the mostly vacant downtown, to the college and the west-end Dairy Queen.

water content in an infant's body is around 75 percent, a fact that invites me to imagine babies as jiggly water balloons with liquid fingers and sweetly sloshing bellies. Wombs, of course, are like water balloons, privately enclosed bodies of water for growing clusters of cells. That our skin keeps water out of our bodies while our cells contain water is mysterious and fascinating to me. To maintain our 60 percent, we have to drink water with our mouths.

We call oceans, seas, lakes, rivers, ponds, creeks, and puddles "bodies of water." A healthy lake doesn't have skin, but I can't help imagining fish, algae, rocks, muck, crayfish, insects, and sunken slimy trash as the cells and organs of a lake's body. I am thankful that my skin keeps slimy trash out of my body and that my filtration system is thus far strong and effective.

THE WELL-SPRING

Jen calls this place a spring, while I call it an artesian well. *No difference*, Jen says. *There's no right or wrong here.* But of course, words being words—being labels—there is a right and a wrong.[3] A *spring,* I learn later, is a place where water from an aquifer emerges naturally at the surface of the earth. An *artesian well* is a place where the water from an aquifer remains subterranean until we drill for it. The water needs

---

3 We use words to differentiate and delimit things, to describe and categorize, to identify and name, to sort the pieces and ideas of our world. Sometimes, sorting via language is helpful for understanding our world and ourselves, but other times we use words to limit people or places, to seal them into little boxes and envelopes. Sometimes we claim labels, and sometimes we fight them.

At what speed or level of exertion does *walk* become *jog* become *run*? Do we divide these acts at a particular per-hour speed, at a particular heart rate or sweat level? Or perhaps at the point when a horse's hooves are all off the ground at once. (Or is that a *gallop*? Maybe a *canter*?)

pressure to send it forth. The three pipes that flow continuously with cold, clear water in Glen Miller Park are from a natural spring.

That a spring is the eye of the landscape is suggested by the Semitic letter *ayin*, which represents an eye, a fountain, a well, or a spring in Hebrew, Aramaic, Arabic, Phoenician, or Egyptian.[4] If a spring is the eye of the landscape, then a spring is a place that sees, that takes in all that surrounds it. It is a point of observation, a place to watch. If a spring is the eye of the landscape, it is also a place that weeps, that flows, that embodies the earth's joy or pain.

THOSE WHO GATHER

In 1806 a group of Quakers came to what is now Richmond, Indiana from, North Carolina. They were the first European American settlers in the area, and the town of about thirty-six thousand people is still home to three separate, active Quaker meeting houses. It grew to be a prosperous industrial town, but like so many Rust Belt and midwestern towns, poverty and decay are widespread now (though many people still live prosperous, comfortable lives here). It is a town where *history* is evident at every turn—from the crumbling railroad buildings and decrepit Victorian homes to the mostly empty downtown and the long-ago record factory, the shell of which was recently restored and hosts weddings and a small Shakespeare festival each summer. The history of this place is rich and interesting, but Jen

---

4 Researching *ayin*, I read of Unicode, of rough versus smooth breathing marks, of glottal stops and diphthongs. The linguistic theories that explain the appearance, sound, and uses of ayin overwhelm me, and then remind me that languages are infinitely complex, and that I will never comprehend their variety, nor the ways that they grow from and reflect our worldviews. Still, I grasp that water and its location have always been essential to life—especially in the desert—and that this letter, this sound—ayin—represents water, fountain, and eye—that these things are connected in language and idea.

and I spend a lot of time talking about what's here *now*. We've been thinking about the places where people gather—the three seasonally operating Dairy Queens (one at each of three compass points) that open each spring and host long lines every night of the summer, the outdoor swimming pool with its brightly colored slides and umbrellas, the growing farmers market in the new downtown park, and this natural spring in Glen Miller Park.

Jen and I sit beside one of the three pipes, sipping water and chatting. A minivan pulls up and a child gets out, crosses to the spring, and fills a single blue plastic bottle that he takes back to the van for help with the screw top. A man arrives with a small metal cart on wheels and fills the bottles that it holds. A group of children arrive with a couple of adults. While the grown-ups fill bottles, one girl drinks directly from the pipe, filling her cupped hands and lifting them to her mouth. A woman with plastic milk jugs strung on a rope chats with us as she shakes the jugs free and fills them one at a time. It's a beautiful afternoon to stop by the spring, but she tells us she comes here for water year-round. *The water at my house is no better in the winter*, she explains. She tells us there are days you have to wait in line to fill your jugs, though today every car that pulls up is able to fill their containers immediately. A man carrying a huge, blue plastic carboy fills the container and carries it back to his car on his shoulder like Atlas carrying the world. A man wearing the blue and gray uniform of the post office arrives and unloads two orange plastic milk crates from the back of his car. Each crate holds three or four plastic milk jugs. The water is for his parents, he tells us. They're on well water and don't like the taste of it. They purchase bottled water for drinking, he says, but they use the spring water for their coffee maker, and he uses it for his fish tank. *After it warms up*, he says, with a laugh. *This water's pretty cold.* His parents used to come here themselves, but they can't get out anymore, so he does it for them. Everyone who comes is reusing old, plastic containers, and I think of all the plastic they keep out of the landfill by coming here instead of buying newly bottled factory water.

The whole time we've been sitting here, we've been sipping water from our own bottles and listening to the sound of constantly running water. Now we both have to pee, so we snap a few photos of the spring, the bridge, the trees, the creek and hillsides, the old iron signpost that is missing its sign, and head off to find the bathrooms.

HISTORIC RICHMOND, INDIANA, FACEBOOK PAGE
9:20 AM, SATURDAY, APRIL 14–FRIDAY, APRIL 20

Shena: I'm interested in the history and stories about the spring in Glen Miller Park. Is there any folklore that surrounds it?

Derrick: It's been said that if you drink the water you will never leave Richmond lol.

At first, I'm disappointed at this response. I wanted magic. I wanted stories. But instead, just this folklore cliché, one of those things that people say about every place—if you don't dump the sand out of your shoes, if you don't take a rock, if you pick a flower, if you swim in the lake or the river or the pool, you'll never leave this place. You'll be stuck forever. It's magic, I suppose, but reported too many times to spark my imagination, too commonplace. But then the responses to Derrick begin to accumulate, and they capture something else about this place, about how people feel about it.

Jeanne: I really like this saying, and there is a truth in it. I don't live there anymore, couldn't wait to get out, but there is something about it from the past that I can't let go. Having said that, you couldn't pay me to move back. But there is something about what it used to be that will always be in my heart.

Johnny: You just answered a question for me! Now I know why I always end up back here! Hahaha!

Derrick: My theory is that Richmond has become an inescapable black hole :)

Johnny: It has to be haha! I've lived in Tennessee, Colorado, and all over Indiana, plus drove a semi for 15 years, and here I am, back in Richmond! :)

Rose: @Jeanne, I know the feeling. I left at the age of 19 and still consider Richmond my home. I find myself really missing my roots. I, too, would never go back there to live, but I would love to visit.

Alice: Untrue, lol. I did [escape]. We now live in Virginia.

Derrick: You may not recognize it, @Rose. Better to keep your memories and ignore the present.

Rose: @Derrick, I'm not afraid of change. The last time I was there, it had changed, but it was still Richmond.

Jeanne: @Rose, don't go back. It's bad. Just live with your memories.

I wonder if they're right—if Richmond's best or most prosperous days are forever behind it, if one is better off remembering the "good old days" and staying away. As for me, I've been here three years now. I've gulped that flavorless water a handful of times. But my days here are numbered.[5]

Harry: The spring is part of an aquafer that flows from Canada to Florida. The water emerges (springs) several countless times through several states. These springs occur when the narrowing of the underground rock forces it upward. I have been in the bottled water business for 40 years.

Michael: Used to go out there with grandpa every week and fill 3 or 4 reused Miller milk house jugs. He always had a few gallons in his fridge!

Lynn: The original land purchase was by the Charles Family and the springs on their property were important to them and their neighbors. Some of the folklore is about the Charles Home being on the Underground Railroad for this part of Indiana.

Jane: We used to get drinks of water from the spring on the backside going out to Hayes Road. I don't know if it dried up or what, and my grandmother, Jeanette H., only drank water from the spring at the bottom of the hill. She was a very healthy woman.

I wonder if the water from the spring is actually more pure or healthy than the water from my kitchen sink. I try to research the quality of

5 Or have I jinxed myself to somehow remain forever, literally or figuratively? At the end of June, I'm off to upstate New York for a new job. I won't read every post on the Historic Richmond, Indiana, Facebook page, but I doubt I'll unfollow it, either. Will I, unexpectedly, leave a piece of my heart in Richmond, Indiana? (Will the water keep me here somehow?)

Richmond's municipal water, but the statistics and measurements are unfamiliar language for me. I know nothing about the types of particulates that are harmful, nor the ways that they are measured. Richmond's water passes the official muster, but that's what they're saying about the water in Flint, Michigan, these days too, and people there still report that it runs brown from their sinks, that they won't bathe in it, much less drink it. Public water isn't tested in individual houses, anyway. There is no acceptable amount of lead exposure for children, but the legal limits are 15 ppm.

The water from the spring tastes like nothing to me, while water from my home tap tastes metallic. But what does it mean if water tastes like nothing? For three summers when I was in college, I led backpacking trips at a summer camp in Colorado. I drank iodine-treated water at least four days a week during those summers. The chemically treated water dyed any bottle brown and tasted terrible, but I got used to that flavor too. It became neutral to me. It became the flavor of nothing, and it was the iodine that made the water safe for me to drink.

Patricia: We used to have family reunions there.

Patsy: There used to be two places to get water at Glen Miller. Now only one. I have photos of my boys getting water at the one [that is] no longer there. I'm going to go to Glen Miller Park soon and get some spring water.

Gunty: This is when they built the stone bridge. It was an arch bridge. At a later date it was reconfigured to its current state.

I study this postcard, doubtful that it depicts the spot where I sat with Jen on Friday. There are many more trees in this image than there are now. I wonder if this is a different bridge in the park, maybe the one farther down-creek toward the duck pond. But in the end, I think Gunty's right. The stone pillars are the same stone pillars that Jen and I climbed on. We wondered what had been atop the iron fixtures until I found a few clipped wires and I surmised there had once been lamps, maybe round white globes. As Gunty points out, the bridge is no longer arched, but it is still built from the round cobblestones.

Judy: I used to love the stone chair that sat just up the hill from the main spring. We were always told that it was a wishing chair, through the 30s, 40s, 50s, 60s . . . now it's completely gone.

Dianne: I have forgotten about this chair. Wonder what happened to it?

Judy: It disappeared stone by stone, as in vandalism. :)

Shena: What did it look like, @Judy? How big? Did you make many wishes there? I have never heard about it, but it sounds sweet.

Judy: @Shena, it was built as a sort of big square chair using those pretty round stones like the bridge is made from. Two people could sit side by side (yes, I went there with dates :)). The seat part was flat cement. Because mother had gone there as a child, we went often too, and made lots of wishes in the 50s/60s. I took my daughter in the 70s. As a teen/ young adult, I would normally wish for world peace, so I guess the chair didn't "work." It does make me sick that it was vandalized. It was lovely.

Shena, Dianne, Rose: ♥

Judy: @Dianne, I had been told they were going to repair it, then it disappeared. History.

Judy: @Shena, I was at the park getting water today and discovered that the base of the chair is still there! I had thought it was ALL gone.

Shena: @Judy, Wow! I wonder if it could be rebuilt. Thanks for the update. I'll have to look for it next time I'm there.[6]

---

6 Rebuilding the chair won't bring prosperity back to Richmond. It won't restore the crumbling houses or the greenhouses full of roses, the lost industry, the bodies of those addicted to opioids, the sense of a future. It won't keep young people here. Or me. But I still think it's a good idea.

A COLD DRINK THAT TASTES OF NOTHING

Most afternoons, I buy an Americano from the coffee kiosk on the college campus where I work. The Americanos there are expensive, but I go there instead of the student coffee co-op, where they are ridiculously cheap, because Tara's Americanos are delicious, and Tara lets me add my own hot water, so the ratio is always right. Plus, the kiosk has half-and-half, while the student co-op only has milk. But I also go to the kiosk because I like talking to Tara. She's about the same age as me, and grew up here in Richmond. Occasionally, in the midst of our small talk, I get a glimpse of her life away from work, of the things she cares about, even though our exchanges are brief. When I go for an Americano and Tara's on break, or out sick, I'm disappointed. Sometimes I even go to the student co-op then, willing to sacrifice the half-n-half to save money and say hi to a student or two. I guess these small moments of conversation are part of my coffee addiction.

Recently I bought a new travel mug from Tara because one of my favorite students—Maddie, a sustainability major—has become, by no fault of her own, my ecological conscience. Every time I use a plastic fork or buy coffee in a paper cup, it is as if a mini-Maddie alights on my shoulder, shaking her head with disappointment. In the weeks since I purchased the travel mug, if I forget it, I imagine Maddie's disappointment as well as the heap of paper cups I have used this year, piled high in a landfill, vultures circling above the un-natural hill where the trash is compacted so tightly that even organic matter can't decompose.

When I tell Tara why I bought the travel mug, she tells me that her daughter, a senior in high school, has recently sworn off the bottled water she grew up drinking. Until last summer, Tara and her daughter lived in the country, and the well water tasted gross, so Tara bought cases of bottled water for them to drink. They moved into town last summer, and Tara's daughter has sworn off plastic bottles. Now she and Tara fill reusable jugs at the spring in Glen Miller Park, a task Tara remembers doing with her grandmother when she was a girl, and now does on her way to or from her weekend job at the hardware store. She goes to the spring to avoid using plastic bottles but also because the water is better there than the water at her house.

Sustainability, flavor, health, sense of community, and some nebulous, romantic idea of rural self-reliance: these are Jen's and my hypotheses about why people visit the spring, and Tara's story confirms some of these ideas. I think people go to the spring because they've always gone, because they went with their parents or their grandparents, and because they used to sit on a stone chair beside the spring and wish for world peace. I think they go to the spring because it's an act that connects them to people they have known and loved. They go because filling a jug of water from a metal pipe in the park seems rustic and pure and healthy.[7]

And maybe some people also go to the spring for the same reason I go to Tara's coffee kiosk: because the spring is a place where people connect with other people, those with whom they share this town, this county, this state. At the spring, we rub our hands together to warm them while the jugs fill, or we splash the cold water on our faces under the new, hot sun of April, or in the sticky heat of August. We hold our bottles to the pipe and wait for them to fill. It's something people have done in Richmond since Richmond can remember, and it's something that we do now, still. The wishing

7 Even if the level of Total Dissolved Solids doesn't support that feeling as factual. I haven't tested the water, and I doubt many of the people who fill jugs there have. Most of us willingly, blindly, believe in the healthfulness of that water, or we believe it can't be worse than the water that flows from the pipes of our old houses.

chair is gone, along with the acres and acres of greenhouses where commercial roses once grew, along with the lawn mower factory, and the piano factory, and the recording studio. The park around the spring is overgrown and sometimes overwhelmed with dead trees and fallen branches, but people still come to the spring for water, and the water still flows. And we chat with each other, and we tip a bottle of cold, clear water to our lips, and we drink from the eye of this particular landscape.

OF GLASS, LIGHT, AND ELECTRICITY

It must be beautiful, if you cannot read.

—George Bernard Shaw upon seeing the
neon of Times Square for the first time.[1]

1. PARTY TRICK, 1880s

First came Geissler tubes, glass spirals and bulbs and loop-de-loops
filled with gas. Add an electrode spark, and the tube glows orange or
blue or white or yellow, depending on which gas it contains (neon,
argon, mercury vapor). A Geissler tube balanced on a fulcrum and,
like a toy top, a push or a motor set it spinning. It became a blur of
light, demonstrating Persistence of Vision, the way fan blades on a
summer afternoon become a circle instead of four separate blades
pushing the stuffy air around. The way hummingbird wings whir in
rapid motion as they hold the bird's tiny body aloft.[2] If it contains

---

1 Neil Postman. *Amusing Ourselves to Death: Public Discourse in the Age of Show
Business* (New York: Penguin Books, 2005).

2 In Mexico, dead hummingbirds—*chuparosas*—are caught and killed, packaged in
paper tubes with tassels to match their feathers. Quick and small, with ruby feathers,
or magenta, green, or gold, or blue: the hummingbird dances on air, seeking sweetness, always moving on. A finger offered as a perch. A flower. *Beauty, don't you tire
of your own whirring heartbeat? Rest here, sweet one, and drink.* A swift fist, a squeeze,
wings and throat pressed tight until its breath stops. The purr of its heart slows then

mercury, a spinning Geissler tube glows blue. It is a supernatural orb, a sci-fi Tinkerbell filled with brilliant sadness, warning of crocodiles and sentient robots. A spinning Geissler tube is uncatchable and bright. A single, clumsy finger would stop it—the colors leaping toward your finger—but who are you to stop light and motion?

2. THE LIQUEFACTION OF AIR, 1902

It was Frenchman Georges Claude who figured out how to cool, compress, and expand air and to separate and store nitrogen, oxygen, and argon in their liquid states. Claude mined the air for elements and learned to bottle them. Every schoolkid learns that solids are the coldest state of matter, followed by liquids, and that gases are the warmest state of matter, swirling invisibly like ghosts or God. That every gas can be a solid if it is cooled and condensed enough.[3] Conversely, every solid can be heated, expanded until it melts, boils, and rises as gas. It's basic science, sure—elementary—but I admit that the facts of science elude me (vaporize, drift) when I imagine that this air I breathe—this dull, invisible, Rust Belt air—can become something that sloshes, or even something that breaks. This midwestern air that smells like dog food on Mondays, cookies on Fridays, and petrochemicals late at night is also oxygen, carbon dioxide, argon,

stops. They're sold in *botanicas* in Mexico, smuggled in boxes and backpacks, in rolls of socks, in water bottles and cans labeled *frijoles* across the border to the US They're said to capture that elusive one you love, the heart of the one who moves too beautifully, too swiftly for you to charm her (like light, she is fleeting). But if you stop the whirring heart, if you still the spinning tube of light, you cannot keep its energy. Stilled, it vanishes, or becomes something else entirely: a charm wrapped in paper, brittle bones and feathers, an empty tube of glass, dull in daylight.

3 For some gases, the freezing point is so far below frostbite it is unfathomable, a temperature we cannot conceive of with our human fingers or teeth or snow-coated whiskers. The freezing point of helium, for example, is -458°F. It is impossible to solidify helium at atmospheric pressure.

nitrogen, and neon. In through the nose, it is suddenly substantial, material. It fills my lungs, but I take it for granted. That *air* is made of sortable elements, that air is *mine-able*, seems supernatural, magical, metaphorical. But liquid neon was a by-product of the liquefaction of air. Claude cooled the air enough that he could pour its elements into glass tubes, and neon signs were born.[4]

4 Georges Claude is sometimes called the Edison of France. In addition to liquefying air and inventing neon tubes, he discovered how to stabilize acetylene so it could be shipped without exploding, and during WWI, he liquefied chlorine gas, which allowed the French to fight back against German attacks. He developed a sound detection system for locating enemy guns, and spent years trying to harness ocean water to generate steam power (this project was fraught with failure and eventually devoured his fortune).

Claude's 1960 *New York Times* obituary also credits him with the development of fluorescein dye. In its crystal form, fluorescein looks like chili powder, deep red and crumbly, but dispersed in water it glows bright green and yellow. Pilots carried it in pouches, and if they crashed over the ocean, air rescuers were able to spot them floating in the vibrant patch of water below. I want it to be true that Claude invented fluorescein because there is a lovely associative logic in one man inventing both neon signs and dye that sets ocean water aglow for the sake of rescuing people. But besides the obituary, I cannot find another source that credits Claude with the invention of fluorescein dye. It seems that it was the Germans who first used fluorescein to rescue crashed pilots, and to make matters worse, Claude was sentenced to life in prison for voluntarily collaborating with Germany during their WWII occupation of France. He was a royalist who supported France's wartime anti-Semitic Vichy government. He openly published propaganda in support of the Nazis. In 1950, after a group of French scientists argued for his freedom on the basis of his contributions to science, Claude was released from prison under the condition that he would not pursue any further scientific work. Claude made signs that shine in darkness, contributed to ecologically sustainable methods of harnessing energy for electricity, and also had a mind filled with shadows and anti-Semitism. (Will this knowledge diminish my love for neon? Will I now think of this darkness every time I see a glowing sign?)

After every visionary act, time rolls on. And over time, some of us cloud our brightness with our darkness, and some of us entirely extinguish what once glowed. (*I am not one to pray, but: let me know what is light, and let me be light, and let me kindle light—today and tomorrow and tomorrow and tomorrow.*)

3. THE STORY OF A SIGN: PACKARD CARS

The first neon sign in the United States was in Los Angeles, of course, purchased from Georges Claude for the Packard car company in 1923. The word *PACKARD* was scrawled in red cursive script (framed with blue) and glowed over the City of Angels at the corner of 7th and Flower, shining like a halo in the dry, black night. Cars pulled to the side of the road so the drivers could admire it. *Liquid fire*, they called it. It was an emblem of the future.[5]

5 And this is the persistent story of the first neon sign in the U.S., but like many of our most persistent stories, it is untrue. Historian Dydia DeLyser sought primary sources to corroborate the story. She looked for a photograph of the sign, or of the traffic jams it purportedly induced, but photographs of the corner of 7th and Flower reveal that the sign wasn't there until 1925—not 1923 (Catherine Saillant, "Pair Sheds New Light on L.A.'s Claim to Neon Fame," *Los Angeles Times*, December 3, 2013). Neon signs glowed on the East Coast by 1924. But does it matter if we tell each other a story about the Packard sign as the first neon this side of the Atlantic? It's a good story, a magical story, like a scene from a movie, all those cars pulled over and lined up to see the shining, candy-colored letters. And at this point, how will we ever know which sign was truly first? Does it change anyone's life or livelihood to tell it wrong, to tell it right? Los Angeles, after all, is a city always angled toward the future, for better or worse, and the first neon sign is a part of that. If the first neon sign this side of the Atlantic glowed, instead, in New York, does it change the way we think of L.A.?

But DeLyser's discovery—her debunking—reminds me, again, that history is fraught with human error—that sometimes we tell a story for selfish aims, to sell more cars, to make ourselves look good, to win elections, or to erase something ugly we'd rather forget. Even persistent myths can be wrong, can squeeze a story too narrowly, reshaping it, and so, yes, it matters.

So how can I revise this (hi)story for accuracy? The Packard sign was a novelty, even if it was not the first one. It probably did stop some traffic, would certainly have turned some heads. The sight of it would have set peoples' imaginations whirling toward a future in which cities were full of flash and gleam and candy glow, a time when electricity and light would be harnessed by language and glass, and the answers to every question would rest like mints on our tongues.

4. YESCO: THE YOUNG ELECTRIC SIGN COMPANY[6]

Thomas Young was born on May 26, 1895, in Sunderland, England. When he was still an infant, his family converted to the Church of Jesus Christ of Latter-day Saints, and so he knew no other life, no other church nor God. And faith, of course, transcends choice for those who have it. He considered himself lucky, elect.

Sunderland means a place where the land divides. It is on the northeast coast, nestled against the North Sea. But Thomas Young and his family left that place, boarded a ship in Liverpool and sailed to Montreal, then boarded a train and rolled across the continent to Ogden, Utah, the Mormon promised land of dust and salt and cottonwood trees. It was 1910 or '11 when Thomas Young arrived in a green train car. He was fifteen years old, thin, and not yet strong, hogging a window seat, his eyes full of mountains and the black smoke of the train. The buildings in his new town were built of red brick and gray stone. There was not even a lake in sight, and it was weeks before he found himself standing beneath a waterfall, half of the thin stream blowing off before it reached the bottom of its fall.

The Mormons had been settling in the Salt Lake valley along the Wasatch Front for over fifty years by the time Young arrived. There must have been fruit trees already, and the pale spires of temples piercing the horizon, white against the backdrop of mountains on all sides. The streets of Ogden marched north and south and east and west in perfectly gridded blocks, moving like armies outward from the Temple. Already it had been decades since teams of oxen hauled tremendous blocks of granite from Cottonwood Canyon to Temple Square in Salt Lake City, forty miles south of Ogden, where the Temple of temples still stands. So Tom Young would be an American, a westerner.

6 http://www.yesco.com/company/take-a-tour-back-through-history/.

He got his start hand-painting signs for others, and when he first founded his own company, he was known for making coffin plaques and hand-painting in gold leaf on windows. He had a steady hand and a graceful brush, and in his free time he painted landscapes in oil on canvas, mountains and trees and the seascapes he remembered from his youth in England.

Neon doesn't require a steady hand or skill with a brush, but rather a flame and the controlled bending of glass tubes. The gas glows against tubes coated with phosphorous. A glass bender solders the electrodes to the end, fixes the letters to a metal frame. It was in neon that Thomas Young made his name.

By the 1950s, his company was bending the tubes that would become some of the most famous neon signs in the U.S.: The brother cowboys Vegas Vic and Wendover Will, The Stardust Motel and the Circus Circus Downtown Spectacular. They didn't own it at the beginning, but they soon acquired Welcome to Fabulous Las Vegas. YESCO[7] is behind them all.

7 It's a common misnomer that young rattlesnakes don't know how to control their venom—that they're snappier and bitter-fanged, afraid, and so quick to bite. Small rattlers are hard to see, low and slender in the grass. Their rattles are not yet loud. We fail to hear their warnings, so they strike at our ankles. At the ranch where I wrote for a month one summer, we wore boots and long pants when we walked in the field, though it was July and terribly hot.

One afternoon, Mike, the groundskeeper, caught a young rattlesnake between the blades of a hedge clipper. He held it up for my camera, clamped and dangling and broken and dead. *Fearsome little thing*, he said. *These little ones bite with the full juices.* I didn't argue, but it's an old wives' tale, another one of those persistent myths. All snakes, young or old, small or large, when they bite, do so with all they've got.

Rattlesnake venom, like young electricity: how it might splinter and spasm and bloom. Young electricity: just born, and now, somehow, trapped on its way from the sun to the leaves and the dirt of the earth. Young electricity poured into glass tubes, now glowing like a brand-new star, bright hot blue, like my heart on a good day.

When a storm rolls in across rangeland, you can see it from miles away. The sky is a violet bruise. Clouds curdle like miso in broth. That summer, I stood atop a hill, a mile from shelter. I was the tallest thing for miles. Still, I paused to compose the

5. THE STORY OF A SIGN:
WELCOME TO FABULOUS LAS VEGAS

In 1959 Betty Willis designed the famous Welcome to Fabulous Las Vegas sign, and Las Vegas has been fabulous ever since.[8] The average lifespan of a sign in Vegas in ten years, but Willis's sign still shines at the edge of town, as well as on the back of playing cards and on the faces of keychains, on postcards and T-shirts and souvenir shot glasses. If Willis had trademarked the now iconic sign, she may have grown rich collecting royalties, or it may have been just another sign, blinking in the desert night until it became unfashionable, faded, and bland, only to be shipped off, filaments busted, to the junkyard or the neon museum. Tour bus drivers tell their passengers—Europeans, Japanese, midwestern Americans, everyone—that it is the most recognized sign in the world. Each letter of the word WELCOME glows red, the letters resting within white circles—silver dollars, Willis said, representing the Silver State. Above the sign, a starburst is the twinkling star of the nuclear era—a "googie." Conjuring showgirls and endless nights, cocktails and big wins and blinking lights, it is extraordinary and mythical.

Betty Willis is a distinctly 1950s name. Betty, they say, was direct and confident and spoke with the tight-lipped, flat, casual speech of a westerner. In later life, she had a gray-white cap of curls. Willis was born in Overton, Nevada, northeast of Las Vegas, north of Lake Mead, near Valley of Fire State Park. On Google Street

shot: yellow grasses bending, a glimmer of light between the clouds and the jagged line of mountains in the distance. I took the photos, and then I ran downhill and lay facedown in the grass, waiting for the lightning to pass (electricity neither young nor old, and the snakes would be sheltering underground). I lay there and waited for the hail.

8 Fabulous (adj.): Extraordinary. Especially extraordinarily large. Amazingly good; wonderful. Having no basis in reality; mythical.

View, I find the scoured brightness of her desert town, cinderblock structures and palm trees, wide pale roads and trailer homes. An Ace Hardware, a Napa Auto Parts, camper trailers with porches, and a military tank parked forever in the center of town, a small flag flying high from its frame. But at the edge of town, roads lead to red rocks with foot trails running between them. Blue skies sear above rocks striped pink and white, like bacon marbled with fat. Betty Willis was born in Overton in 1923, but in 1942—at nineteen—she moved to L.A. for art school. The war was on, and art school hardly seems like contributing to the war effort. How (a)typical was Betty, I wonder, a woman moving to the city alone, designing ads for Fox West Coast Theaters, then returning to Las Vegas and working for the courthouse until she began designing signs for Western Neon?

Willis died in Overton in 2015. I imagine the town through her eyes, accustomed to a palette of blue skies and pale green plants, red rocks and wide gray expanses of dirt. Her lungs used to the cool air of morning and the oven breath of afternoon, the drone of an airplane interrupting the silence.

6. GLASS BENDER

1. Glass bender: a noun in the bottom 10 percent for frequency of use

2. Glass bender: a worker who shapes the discs for clocks, speedometers, headlights

3. Glass bender: a worker or artist who shapes the tubes for neon signs and fuses them to the electrodes that spark their glow

4. [To go on a] *glass bender*: to drive through the city for hours for the sole purpose of admiring the neon: Shangri La. Chop Suey. Bar Deluxe. Girls, Girls, Girls. Palm trees and martini glasses. Open. Closed.

5. Glass bender: a distorting lens. The way, when you fill your eyes with the light of a neon sign and then turn away, your vision fills with the blackness that buzzed around the sign. The brightness of neon overshadows the metal on which the glass tubes hang, erases the cheap stools inside the bar, the sagebrush and mica of the desert, the blowing trash, and stars.

7. THE STORY OF A SIGN: OQUIRRH APARTMENTS

On 3rd South and 4th East, in Salt Lake City, across from Ichiban, the sushi restaurant in an old church, stands the apartment building named Oquirrh. Plain white, three stories tall, holds maybe six or twelve apartments. I have never been inside, but I always stop to admire its neon sign. Oquirrh is the name of the mountains that form the western lip of the city's bowl. A creek runs from the canyon in the north and joins the Jordan River in the west, funneling along the flats between the city and the Oquirrhs. *Oquirrh* is a Goshute word meaning "sitting wood," perhaps for the trees that flank the mountains, though these aren't even as thick as the forests of the Wasatch Range to the east of the city. The Goshutes lived in the valley to the west of the mountains, on open rangeland. Among other things, they ate lizards and ants and pine nuts. The word *oquirrh* makes me wish to hear their language: so many consonants, the click of the *Q*, the buzz and whoosh of *r*'s, the wing-lift of the *h*. OQUIRRH glows pink over the door of the apartment building, simple capital letters buzzing through the night, flickering since the time when neon named most of the city's apartment buildings: Peter Pan, Belvedere, Bel Wines, Embassy Arms, Picadilly, Bigelow, Castle Heights. But none catch my eye like the pink glow of the Oquirrh, whirring like wings and dreams in the dark.

8. NEON IS NOBLE

Ne on the periodic table, atomic number 10. It was discovered by Sir William Ramsay and Morris Travers in 1889. Neon is a noble gas, meaning it's stable and rarely—if ever—reacts with other gases. The list of noble gases includes neon, helium, argon, xenon, krypton, and radon, though these last three more recently have been found to form compounds with other elements after all, polluting the term noble, or losing their isolationism.

The word *neon* comes from Greek for "new," though of course, when it was named there was nothing new about its existence. Neon had been there, in the air around us, in the veritable forever. What was new was our identification of it, our isolation of it, our ability to name it. Odorless, colorless, monatomic, with low chemical reactivity—neon is a silent, invisible, nonreactive, inert gas.

It is, apparently, noble to be non-reactive, to be disinterested in entanglements. To be aloof. It seems to follow, then, that to be highly reactive or volatile, is to be ignoble.[9]

Neon floats above it all, a steady glow within glass tubes, until it reaches midlife—say the 1960s to the 1980s—when, despite its nobility, neon signs are deemed an emblem of the tawdry, of barrooms and prostitution, gambling, fast food, late night carousing, peep shows, and pornography. Neon provides the back-alley light of drug deals, casual affairs, and knife fights. But now, in old age, as the

---

9 I cannot help but love the word *ignoble*. A strange word, with a *g* where one might expect an *n* (innoble, unnoble, annoble). *IGnoble!* Like Iggy Pop in the passenger seat, lusting for life as the car glides through the city. Like eggs and fizzing sulfur. Like fireworks and smoke. There's something about the roll and bubble of the word that just feels good in my mouth and in my ear, like the snap of bubble gum, a mouthful of pop rocks, candy-bright, sugary, and loud. To be ignoble is to be shabby, to be crass, dishonest, savage, dishonorable, vile, and dastardly. Despite my love for the word, I don't strive for ignobility of self, nor in gases, friends, bosses, or world leaders.

signs blink out and find their ways to museums, neon is again, like always, jewel-gleam in darkness.

9. THE STORY OF A SIGN: WENDOVER WILL

Filmmakers say you can't fake the neon glow of the Vegas Strip. If you want the Strip in your film, you've got to film it on the Strip. There's no studio magic that can render it, no Photoshop-filter or green screen. There's only the Real Thing.

I haven't spent much time in Vegas, but I know you can't fake the smell of sage in the darkness, the glow on the horizon that is Wendover, Nevada, when I take a ranch exit and get out of the car in the dark to pee. Cooling, the car engine ticks, and I lean back on the hood to look at the sky for a minute. I fill my lungs with spring night air. The sky seems blacker in the desert, and maybe it is: there are fewer particles of humidity reflecting light. And there are few lights to begin with.

But I get back in the car, and soon enough, a blaze of neon and flashing lights as Wendover arises on the border of Nevada and Utah, the divide between sinners and saints. Wendover Will, a sixty-three-foot-tall neon cowboy, commissioned in 1952 by the Stateline Casino. Will is the brother to the more famous Vegas Vic, 1951, whose clothes are more streamlined—checkered shirt, cigar—and whose body language is more casual and confident—he points with his thumb. If you're driving east through Wendover, Will says *This Is the Place*. If you're driving west, he pivots his arm: *This Way, This Way, To Where the West Begins*.

The West begins in St. Louis, at the Arch, and in Kansas City, in Denver, and on the Continental Divide. But it begins, too, in West Wendover, Nevada, after the long stretch of the salt flats (where the only sound is the crunch of the crystals beneath your feet, and in daylight the mountains are blue in the distance.) Here, in Wendover, the West begins when you step from the restaurant side, in Utah, to the casino side, in Nevada, an invisible line drawn through the velvet night. Wendover Will swings his neon arm, blinking *This way. This way.* To sagebrush and cowboys. To snowcaps and missile tests. To desolation and sky and sand and ocean. To shoes dangling from the branches of solitary trees. To *cholla* blooming in dirt. To rusted tin cans left by the miners. To vultures and glinting mica. To frosted mornings and grass pressed flat by the bodies of deer. To valleys dammed and flooded. To jugs of water left by the side of the road (don't think of the bodies that don't make it far enough to tip that jug to their lips and drink). *This way. This way.* To everything you'll ever love.[10]

10. EMBLEMS, ICONS, AGING

But what's my thing with neon, anyway? I've never bent glass. I don't understand the elements of air, or what it means to be noble. I no longer live in the West, where the signs that are iconic to me glow against the night sky until the sun rises and they stop their buzzing and chattering and rest, innocuous and dull in the sunlight, which is, after all, brighter and more powerful than gas in glass tubes.

Maybe it's that neon signs are emblems of the cities that I miss, the signs that drew me through the dark. We know our cities by their neon, whether we realize it or not. Denver, the city I still call home, though I haven't lived there in years, is the shining letters of Olinger's Mortuary, the Bluebird Theater, Denver Diner, Pete's Kitchen, the Mayan Theater, Union Station: Travel-By-Train, and Jesus Saves at the Rescue Mission (crossword style: the middle S of Jesus—across— is the first S of Saves—down).

---

10   But you'll move east, then east again, and maybe east again.

And like the Packard sign in Los Angeles (1925), neon signs were an emblem of the future, and then, for a time, they meant lurid things, and now they've been replaced by glowing plastic cabinets, painted letters, and LED. bulbs. Today, neon is mostly nostalgia and song lyrics. Neon is raindrops shining on the window, or in the condensation on your bottle of beer.

Maybe it's that neon's arc is my arc, or so it seems, the arc of aging. In youth, we are shiny with promise, but in middle age, we're deemed shabby and washed up, or we know the wrong things—crass and useless things that amount to nothing. And perhaps we are less efficient, but still, we gleam. For the perceptive ones, for those with a sense of curiosity, we might, as we age, glow with the magic of some other time, when men wore felt hats, and women with long fingers knew how to hold their chopsticks, how to wear lipstick, how to channel the energy within themselves so they glowed.

There's not much neon where I live now, this town of forty thousand people in eastern Indiana, but there's a drugstore sign that hangs over a doorway on a side street, blue and white linked letters reading *PHILLIPS REXALL DRUGS*. On summer nights, it shines most deliciously against the blue of the sky. But mostly, I have to look for the glow elsewhere. There's something of sunrise and sunset in neon, and something of neon in sunrise and sunset. Such an extravagance of color and light, the gaudy blaze as day gives way to night, or night to day. Fleeting pink skies, and the deep electric blue of twilight. Just this morning, I watched a streetlight flicker off against a pink and purple sky. The fire faded, and another gray day began, the frozen world blanketed with snow, and my coffee steaming in lamplight beside me. In these fleeting minutes between night and day, everything is magical.

SELECTED BIBLIOGRAPHY

ENDNOTES TO A SEIZURE

Blom, Jan Dirk. *A Dictionary of Hallucination*. New York: Springer, 2010.

Christiansen, Jen. "Pop Culture Pulsar: Origin Story of Joy Division's *Unknown Pleasures* Album Cover." *Scientific American*, February 18, 2105. https://blogs.scientificamerican.com/sa -visual/pop-culture-pulsar-origin-story-of-joy-division-s -unknown-pleasures-album-cover-video/.

Dostoyevsky, Fyodor. *The Idiot*. Translated by David Margarshack. London: Penguin Classics, 1956.

Hitt, Jack. "This Is Your Brain on God." *Wired*, November 1, 1999. https://www.wired.com1999/11 /persinger/?pg=3&topic=&topic_set=.

The Holy Bible. New International Version. Grand Rapids, MI: Zondervan Publishing House, 1984.

Homer. *The Odyssey*. Translated by Richmond Lattimore. New York: Harper Perennial, 1967.

Kumar, David R.; Florence Asilinia, MD; Steven H. Yale, MD; and Joseph J. Mazza, MD. "Jean-Martin Charcot: The Father of Neurology." *Clinical Medicine & Research* 9, no. 1 (March 2011): 46–49.

Landsborough, D. "St. Paul and Temporal Lobe Epilepsy." *The Journal of Neurology, Neurosurgery, and Psychology* 50 (1987): 659–664.

Rilke, Rainer Maria. "For the Sake of a Single Poem," In *The Selected Poetry of Rainer Maria Rilke*, edited and translated by Stephen Mitchell. New York: Vintage Books, 1982.

Temkin, Owsei. *The Falling Sickness: A History of Epilepsy from the Greeks to the Beginnings of Modern Neurology*. Baltimore: Johns Hopkins University Press, 1971.

THE HEALING MACHINE

Bawden, Arthur Talbot. *Matter and Energy: A Survey of the Physical Science*. New York: Henry Holt & Company, 1957.

Duggan, Joe. "The Healing Machines of Nebraska." *Lincoln Journal Star*, January 7, 2006.

Johnson, Ken. "Emery Blagdon: Flights of Fancy from the Artist as Medicine Man." *The New York Times*, January 10, 2008.

Umberger, Leslie. "Emery Blagdon: Properly Channeled." In *Sublime Spaces and Visionary Worlds*: Built Environments of Vernacular Artists, 203–23. New York: Princeton Architecture Press, 2007.

TEN ON POISON

Cockburn, Alexander. "Zyklon B on the US Border." *The Nation*, July 9, 2007. https:/www.thenation.com/article /zyklon-b-us-border/.

Deutsches Spionage Museum. "The 'Bulgarian Umbrella': Examining the Theory of a Spectacular Murder." https://www. deutsches-spionagemuseum.de/en/sammlung /bulgarian-umbrella/.

Everts, Sarah. "The Nazi Origins of Deadly Nerve Gases." *Chemical & Engineering News*, October 17, 2016. https://cen.acs.org /articles/94/i41/Nazi-origins-deadly-nerve-gases.html.

Gutman, Yisrael, and Michael Berenbaum. *Anatomy of the Auschwitz Death Camp*. Bloomington: Indiana University Press in association with The United States Holocaust Memorial, 1994.

Mellan, Ibert, and Eleanor Mellan. *Dictionary of Poisons*. New York: Philosophical Library, 1956.

THIS HUMAN SKIN

American Studies at the University of Virginia. "The Scalp Industry." http://xroads.virginia.edu/~hyper/hns/scalpin/oldfolks.html (site discontinued).

Armstrong, Benjamin G., and Thomas Wentworth. *Early Life Among the Indians: Reminiscences from the Life of Benjamin G. Armstrong*. Ashland, WI: A. W. Bowron, 1892.

Belfast Telegraph. "Knife 'Inside Head for Four Years,'" February 18, 2011.http://www.belfasttelegraph.co.uk/breakingnews/offbeat /knife-inside-head-for-four-years-28590542.html.

Connell, Evan S. *Son of the Morning Star.* San Francisco: North Point Press, 1984.

Custer, Elizabeth B. *Boots and Saddles; or, Life in Dakota With General Custer.* Norman: University of Oklahoma Press, 1961.

Goltz, Herbert C. W. "Michikinakoua." *Dictionary of Canadian Biography,* vol. 5, University of Toronto/Université Laval, 2003–, accessed August 23, 2013. http://www.biographi.ca/en /bio/michikinakoua_5E.html.

Herodotus. *The Landmark Herodotus: The Histories.* Edited by Robert B. Strassler. Translated by Andrea L. Purvis. New York: Anchor Books, 2009.

Huffington Post. "Chinese Man Lives with Knife in Head for Four Years," accessed August 25, 2013. http://www.huffingtonpost. com/2011/02/18/knife-removed-from-chines_n_824999.html (page discontinued).

Inman, Henry. *The Old Santa Fe Trail: The Story of a Great Highway.* London: Macmillan, 1898. Project Gutenberg, 2005, https://www.gutenberg.org/ebooks/7984.

Kidston, Martin J. "Northern Cheyenne Break Vow of Silence." *Helena Independent Record,* June 27, 2005. https://helenair.com/ news/state-and-regional/northern-cheyenne-break-vow-of -silence/article_fcf44c96-cfb6-56f4-9c57-062e944350ce.html.

The Second Book of the Maccabees. https://st-takla.org
/pub_Deuterocanon/Deuterocanon-Apocrypha_El
-Asfar_El-Kanoneya_El-Tanya__9-Second-of-Maccabees.
html#Chapter%207.

Twomy, Steve. "Phineas Gage: Neuroscience's Most Famous
Patient." *Smithsonian Magazine,* January 2010. http://www.
smithsonianmag.com/history-archaeology/Phineas-Gage-
Neurosciences-Most-Famous-Patient.html?c=y&page=1.

Wert, Jeffry D. *Custer: The Controversial Life of George Armstrong
Custer.* New York: Simon and Schuster, 1996.

THE DISTANCE BETWEEN IS AN UNBROKEN LINE

Cixous, Hélène. "The Laugh of the Medusa." Translated by Keith
Cohen and Paula Cohen. *Signs: Journal of Women in Culture and
Society* 1, no. 4 (Summer 1976): 875–93.

Drucker, Johanna. *Figuring the Word: Essays on Books, Writing, and
Visual Poetics.* New York: Granary Books, 1993.

AS A BITCH PACES ROUND HER TENDER WHELPS,
SO GROWLS [MY] HEART

Homer. *The Odyssey.* Translated by S. H. Butcher and A. Lang.
London: Macmillan, 1879.

Munger, Steven D. "The Taste Map of the Tongue You Learned
in School Is All Wrong." Smithsonian.com, May 23, 2017.
https://www.smithsonianmag.com/science-nature/neat
-and-tidy-map-tastes-tongue-you-learned-school-all-wrong
-180963407/#V2LUutSQvq4bRTS6.99.

THE PIGMENT IN THE WALL

Barthes, Roland. *Mythologies*. Translated by Annette Lavers. New York: Hill and Wang, 1984.

Mangla, Ravi. "True Blue: A Brief History of Ultramarine." *Paris Review*, June 8, 2015. https://www.theparisreview.org/blog/2015/06/08/true-blue/.

Traveling in Tuscany. "Piero della Francesca: Madonna del Parto (1459–1467)." http://www.travelingintuscany.com/art/pierodellafrancesca/madonnadelparto.htm.

Tumino, Liana Sofia. *The Strappo Technique*. October 25, 2009. https://www.youtube.com/watch?v=MzCDPDmk3AQ.

A PERFECT TIME TO THINK SILVER

Brakhage, Stan. "Maya Deren." In Film at Wit's End: Eight Avant-Garde Filmmakers. New York: McPherson, 1991.

Deren, Maya. "Amateur Versus Professional," In *Essential Deren*, edited by Bruce R. McPherson. New York: Documentext, 2015.

———— "A Statement of Principles," In *Film Manifestos and Global Cinema Cultures: A Critical Anthology*, edited by Scott Mackenzie, 56–58. Berkeley: University of California Press, 2014.

————, dir. *Maya Deren Experimental Films*. Perf. Maya Deren, Alexander Hammid, Chao Li Chi, Talley Beatty. Louisville, CO: Mystic Fire Video. 1943.

Deren, Maya, Teiji Ito, and Cherel Ito, dir. *Divine Horsemen: The Living Gods of Haiti*. Louisville, CO: Mystic Fire Video, 1985.

Kudlacek, Martina, dir. *In the Mirror of Maya Deren*. Perf. Miriam Arsham, Stan Brakhage, Chao Li Chi, Rita Christiani, Maya Deren. Zeitgeist Films, 2004. DVD.

Nichols, Bill. *Maya Deren and the American Avant-Garde*. Los Angeles: University of California Press, 2001.

Oxford English Dictionary. "Trance." 2010. OED.com.

Sitney, P. Adams. *Visionary Film*. New York: Oxford University Press, 1974.

BY SOOT, BY FLOUR, BY BEETLE TRACK

Abt, Regina, Irmgard Bosch, and Vivienne MacKrell. *Dream Child: Creation and New Life in Dreams of Pregnant Women, Inspired by Marie-Louise Von Franz*. Einsiedeln, Switzerland: Daimon, 2000.

AskDefine. "Define Augury." https://augury.askdefine.com/.

Lawson, Willow. "Sexuality: Your Telltale Fingertips." *Psychology Today,* July 1, 2005. https://www.psychologytoday.com/us /articles/200507/sexuality-your-telltale-fingertips.

Livius, Titus. *The History of Rome: Books 01 to 08*. Translated by D. Spillan, London: Henry G. Bohn, 1853; Project Gutenberg, 2006, https://www.gutenberg.org/files/19725/19725 -h/19725-h.htm.

Occult World. "Urticariaomancy." http://occult-world.com/augury /urticariaomancy/.

Watts, T. M., L. Holmes, J. Raines, S. Orbell, and G. Rieger. "Finger Length Ratios of Identical Twins with Discordant Sexual Orientations." *Archives of Sexual Behavior.* 47, no. 8 (2018): 2435–44. https://doi.org/10.1007/s10508-018 -1262-z.

Wikipedia. "Methods of Divination." Last updated October 6, 2019. https://en.wikipedia.org/wiki/Methods_of_divination.

Wilkinson, Endymion. *Chinese History: A Manual.* 2nd ed. Cambridge, MA: Harvard University Asia Center, 2000.

LIGHT IS A WELL-SHOT ARROW

Atkins, Anna Children. "Drawings for Lamarck's Genera of Shells 1823." *Quarterly Journal of Science, Literature and the Arts,* volume XVI, plate V. London: John Murray, 1823. https://www .flickr.com/photos/photohistorytimeline/25880985413/in /photolist-7do1CE-2e9G3Ym-Fr1Phr-FqQkpJ-xoHcGD -Z6WumB.

Cameron, Julia Margaret. "John Herschel (1815–1879)." commons.wikimedia.org/wiki/John_Herschel#/media/File:Julia _Margaret_Cameron_John_Herschel_(Metropolitan_Museum _of_Art_copy,_restored)_levels.jpg.

Kraft, Alexander. "On the Discovery and History of Prussian Blue." *Bulletin for the History of Chemistry.* 33, no. 2 (2008): 61–67.

Levine, Russell, and Chris Evers. "The Slow Death of Spontaneous Generation (1668–1859)." The National Health Museum. http://webprojects.oit.ncsu.edu/project/bio183de/Black /cellintro/cellintro_reading/Spontaneous_Generation.html.

NASA Science: *Share the Science.* "Solar Pinholes." May 30, 2003.
https://science.nasa.gov/science-news
/science-at-nasa/2003/30may_solareclipse2.

Pollan, Michael. *The Botany of Desire.* New York: Random House,
2002.

Schaaf, Larry. *Sun Gardens: Cyanotypes by Anna Atkins.* Munich,
Germany: Prestel, 2018.

OVERGROWN STAIRWAY

History Detectives: Investigations. "Fiery Cross." 2012. Season 10,
episode 2. Public Broadcasting Services.https://www.pbs.org
/opb/historydetectives/investigation/fiery-cross/.

Lost Richmond. "Starr Piano Factory." Richmond, Indiana:
Morrisson-Reeves Library. https://mrlinfo.org/history
/lostrichmond/starrpiano.htm.

MARCELINE WANTED A BIGGER ADVENTURE

Chilcoate, Avelyn. Quoted in Guinn, *The Road to Jonestown* 48.

Cordell, Rick. Quoted in Guinn, *The Road to Jonestown*, 92.

Guinn, Jeff. *The Road to Jonestown: Jim Jones and Peoples Temple.*
New York: Simon and Schuster, 2017.

Jones, Stephan. "Marceline/Mom." Alternative Considerations of
Jonestown & Peoples Temple. The Jonestown Institute at San
Diego State University. March 16, 2019. https://jonestown.sdsu
.edu/?page_id=32388.

———— Quoted in Guinn, *The Road to Jonestown*, 235.

Kilduff, Marshall, and Phil Tracy. "Inside Peoples Temple," *New West Magazine*, August 1, 1977. jonestown.sdsu.edu/wp-content/uploads/2013/10/newWestart.pdf.

Lindsay, Robert. "How Rev. Jim Jones Gained His Power Over Followers." *New York Times*, November 26, 1978.

Luther, Jeanne Jones. Quoted in Guinn, *The Road to Jonestown*, 51.

Moore, Rebecca. "Before the Tragedy at Jonestown, the People of Peoples Temple Had a Dream." *The Conversation.* November 16, 2018. https://theconversation.com/before-the-tragedy-at-jonestown-the-people-of-peoples-temple-had-a-dream-103151.

Truitt, Jason. "Old Reid Hospital: How Did We Get Here?" Pal-Item.com, July 14, 2017. https://www.pal-item.com/story/news/local/2017/07/14/decline-old-reid-hospital-how-did-we-get-here/467479001/.

PIETÀ

"Robbery Suspect Killed in Richmond, Ind. Restaurant." *Dayton Daily News* October 25, 2012. https://www.daytondailynews.com/news/robbery-suspect-killed-richmond-ind-restaurant/c5Dnd1Vu07hjYWleMMwB4K/.

BLIGHT (DISAMBIGUATION)

"Blight Elimination Program: Cities of Promise Grant Work Plan Report." February 27, 2008. https://www.michigan.gov/documents/dleg/cities_of_promise_blight_elim_240482_7.pdf.

City of Richmond [Indiana] Department of Metropolitan Development. "Blight Elimination Program Presentation." 2014. https://www.richmondindiana.gov/docs /blight-elimination-program.

Michigan Vacant Property Campaign. "New Michigan Blight Elimination: Guidebook for Community and Economic Development." Michigan State University Extension, April 2015. https://www.canr.msu.edu/news/new_michigan_blight_ elimination_guidebook_helps_communities_increase_commun.

Schumann, G.L., and C. J. D'Arcy. "Late Blight of Potato and Tomato." *The Plant Health Instructor*. Updated 2018. https:// www.apsnet.org/edcenter/disandpath/oomycete/pdlessons /Pages/LateBlight.aspx.

Sterpka, Marty. "Cleveland's For-profit Urban Gardens Are Growing." Cleveland.com, July 6, 2009. https://www.cleveland.com /metro/2009/07/clevelands_forprofit_urban_gar.html.

Suffert, Frédéric, Émilie Latxague, and Ivan Sache. "Plant Pathogens as Agroterrorist Weapons: Assessment of the Threat for European Agriculture and Forestry," *Food Security* 1, no. 2 (June 2009): 221–32.

Wikipedia. "Blight (Disambiguation)." https://en.wikipedia.org /wiki/Blight_(disambiguation).

A SPRING IS THE EYE OF THE LANDSCAPE

Find a Spring. Glen Miller Park Spring, Richmond, Indiana. http:// www.findaspring.com/locations/north-america/usa /glen-miller-park-spring-richmond-indiana/.

Hebrew for Christians. "The Letter Ayin." http://www
.hebrew4christians.com/Grammar/Unit_One/Aleph-Bet/Ayin/
ayin.html.

Historic Richmond Indiana Photos. Facebook. https://www
.facebook.com/groups/HistoricRichmondIndianaPhotos
/permalink/1239705236163974/.

Indiana American Water. "2018 Annual Water Quality Report,"
accessed 12/10/19. http://www.amwater.com/ccr/richmond.pdf

USGS. "The Water in You: Water and the Human Body." https://
www.usgs.gov/special-topic/water-science-school/science
/water-you-water-and-human-body?qt-science_center
_objects=0#qt-science_center_objects.

OF GLASS, LIGHT, AND ELECTRICITY

Benjamin, Jordan. "Are Baby Rattlesnakes Really More Dangerous
Than Adults?" *Wild Snakes Education and Discussion*, April 24,
2018. https://wsed.org/baby-snake-venom-myth/.

Bright, William. "Oquirrh." *Native American Placenames of the
United States*. Norman, University of Oklahoma Press, 2004.

City of West Wendover. "Wendover Will History Page." https://
www.westwendovercity.com/what-s-new/wendover-will
/wendover-will-history-page.

Ebersole, Rene. "Inside the Black Market Hummingbird Love
Charm Trade." *National Geographic Online*, April 18, 2018.
https://www.nationalgeographic.com/news/2018/04
/wildlife-watch-illegal-hummingbird-trade-love-charm
-mexico-witchcraft/.

NBC News. "Betty Willis, Designer of 'Welcome to Fabulous Las Vegas' Sign, Dies." April 21, 2015. https://www.nbcnews.com /news/us-news/betty-willis-designer-welcome-fabulous-las -vegas-sign-dies-n345386.

New York Times. "Georges Claude, Inventor, Dies; Creator of Neon Light Was 89: Maker of Gas Used in World War I Was Sentenced as Collaborator With Nazis." May 24, 1960.

Postman, Neil. *Amusing Ourselves to Death: Public Discourse in the Age of Show Business.* London: Penguin Books, 2005.

Saillant, Catherine. "Pair Sheds New Light on L.A.'s Neon Claim to Fame." *Los Angeles Times*, December 3, 2013.

Stewart, Doug. "Neon." Chemicool, October 17, 2012. https:// www.chemicool.com/elements/neon.html.

Yesco. "Take a Tour Back Through History." https://www.yesco .com/company/take-a-tour-back-through-history/.

ACKNOWLEDGMENTS

I wrote the essays collected here across a decade of my life, as I moved from the northwest corner of the country to the northeast, with many stops in between. Seeing them all together now, I am grateful to the many people who have contributed to this book, in ways large and small.

Thank you to *Permafrost* at the University of Alaska and to Elena Passarello, for choosing my manuscript so it could become a book. Thank you to the University of Alaska Press, especially Nate Bauer and Krista West, who have been patient with my every error and request.

Thank you to the editors and publications who first published these essays, sometimes in slightly different form: "Endnotes to a Seizure" in *Black Warrior Review*, "The Healing Machine" in *Conjunctions*, "This Human Skin" in *Better: Culture and Lit*, "The Distance Between Is An Unbroken Line" on the website *Mapping Salt Lake City*, "As a Bitch Paces Round Her Tender Whelps, So Growls [My] Heart" in *The Collagist*, "A Perfect Time to Think Silver" in *Eleven Eleven*, "By Soot, By Flour, By Beetle Track" in *Gulf Coast*, "Ten on Poison" in *Bellingham Review*, "Light Is a Well-Shot Arrow" in *Western Humanities Review*, "Overgrown Stairway: Richmond, Indiana" in *Cincinnati Review*, "Pietà: Richmond, Indiana" in *AGNI*

Online, "Marceline Wanted a Bigger Adventure" in *True Story*, "Blight (Disambiguation)" in *Halophyte*, and "Of Glass, Light, and Electricity" in *Copper Nickel*.

Thank you to Daniel Weinshenker and Ryan Trauman of Story Center for helping me find the shape for "Pietà," and for introducing me to new ways of sharing stories. Thank you to Maggie Nelson and Ander Monson for choosing my essays as contest winners; it was energizing to know that they had admired something in my work. Thank you to Wayne Koestenbaum for his thoughtful consideration of an early draft of "Endnotes to a Seizure," and to Emily Dyer Barker for getting me walking with renewed sense of purpose on behalf of the Halophyte Collective.

Thank you to my students for helping me think about reading and writing (and so much more) in new ways every day.

I am infinitely grateful to my colleagues at Cornell College, Earlham College, and Union College. The conversations we have had, the walks we have taken, the books you have suggested, the talks you have given: you have contributed to this book in more ways that I can note.

Thank you again and again to the faculty at the University of Utah. I wrote many of these essays in your classes and all of them under your influence: Melanie Rae Thon, Scott Black, Paisley Rekdal, Craig Dworkin, François Camoin, Michael Mejia, Gretchen Case, Kathryn Bond Stockton, and Lance Olsen.

To my cohort and my friends at the University of Utah and in Salt Lake: thank you for reading drafts of some of these essays and for making them better. Even more, thank you for shared drinks, meals, walks, hikes, and necessary adventures that helped me write. Thank you, V Wetlaufer, Nate Liederbach, Will Kaufman, Andy Farnsworth, Camie Schaefer, Erin Rogers, Erica Plummer, Charles

Plummer, Natanya Ann Pulley, Rachel Hanson, Matthew Nye, Susan McCarty, Danielle Deulen, Shira Dentz, Jacob Paul, Esther Lee, Caren Beilin, Jessica Alexander, Halina Duraj, Anne Royston, Tasha Matsumoto, and Raphael Dagold. Thank you especially to Rachel Marston, Robert Glick, and Catie Crabtree, for everything, especially on the hardest days.

Thank you, Jen Cardinal, for your reliable willingness to talk to strangers. Thank you, Michelle Tong (and Mama and Papa Tong), and thank you, David Woody. Anton DiSclafani and TaraShea Nesbit: my friendships with you two are the golden tickets hidden in the wrapper of this writing life.

Thank you to my sisters, Caitlin and Brigid: you are my earliest companions, my allies and my rivals, my friends. I can't even trace the ways you've shaped me.

And to Jesse, always Jesse, thank you for making dinner, fixing the boiler, trimming junipers, going to the market, and not keeping a tab. Thank you for moving with me, time and again, further and farther east, and for paying a different sort of attention to things, for remembering details, and for feeding my questions with your own questions. Thank you, especially, for getting me away from my desk and my books sometimes.

And finally, thank you, Mom and Dad, for encouraging my reading and writing from the beginning, but even more for showing me that even the dirt in a freshly plowed field is worthy of curiosity and awe. Thank you for giving me the time and space for wonder.

Past winners of *Permafrost Magazine's* Annual Book Prize.
For more info visit *permafrostmag.uaf.edu/contests/*

2014   Adam Tavel, *Plash and Levitation* (Poetry)

2015   Becky Hagenston, *Scavengers: Stories* (Fiction)

2016   Anand Prahlad, *The Secret of a Black Aspie* (Nonfiction)

2017   Gail C. DiMaggio, *Woman Prime* (Poetry)

2018   Roger Wall, *During-the-Event* (Fiction)

2019   Shena McAuliffe, *Glass, Light, Electricity* (Nonfiction)